More Praise for *Present Comfort*

"Julie Yarbrough attends to grief in a way that provides for us all. There is personal, private grief over loss suffered alone. There is also shared, collective grief over the large calamities suffered by all. Grief provides us a way ahead, difficult though it may be. And Julie provides us both thoughtfulness and companionship for the journey. These reflections and resources of the spirit reorient and remind us that we are not alone and not without direction."

–Dr. Gil Rendle, Consultant, Author & Sr. Vice President of the Texas Methodist Foundation (retired), Author of *Quietly Courageous: Leading the Church in a Changing World*

"With the rich resources of Scripture, poetry, and stories, *Present Comfort* is a marvelous exposition of one of the grand themes of the Bible; that "God is with us," especially in the darkest and most difficult times in our lives. This is simply a wonderfully "hope-full" book for all of us in uncertain and challenging seasons in our lives."

–Tom Locke, President, Texas Methodist Foundation

"In her newest book, *Present Comfort*, Julie Yarbrough gives us rich language to understand the complexity of grief. Weaving scripture with personal experience and insights, she invites us not only to face our grief, but to embrace it. In today's climate, *Present Comfort* can be just that: a comforting companion for a weary soul, a reminder that we are not alone as we walk through the valley."

–Lisa Greenwood, Vice President of Leadership Ministry, Texas Methodist Foundation

"In *Present Comfort* Julie Yarbrough eloquently gives voice to the experience of loss, both personal and societal, and provides reassurance of God's steadfast presence in each moment. Individuals and groups alike will find *Present Comfort: Meditations on Modern Loss and Grief* a powerful compendium for working through the layers of grief to find a place of trust and joy we thought unimaginable."

–**Rev. Connie L. Nelson**, Perkins School of Theology, Southern Methodist University

"Julie Yarbrough's extraordinary work invites us to encounter the very presence of God through biblically grounded insights into the nature of grief that engage the mind and touch the heart as she takes us on a journey toward spiritual and emotional wholeness. *Present Comfort* is an essential resource to help us faithfully and deftly navigate the path of life.

–**Dr. Robert Hasley**, Founding Pastor of St. Andrew United Methodist Church, Plano, Texas

"In this exceptional volume of meditations, Julie Yarbrough has provided a fountain of wisdom, insight, honesty, and hope. This book of meditations can be diligently read as a whole volume or digested in daily doses to renew our reliance on God, who is with us as a present comfort in time of grief."

–**Dr. William B. Lawrence**, Professor Emeritus of American Church History, Perkins School of Theology, Southern Methodist University and Research Fellow, Duke Center for Studies in the Wesleyan Tradition

"With each turn of page, readers of *Present Comfort* will come to know Julie as a new friend who has a vulnerable, compassionate, and courageous heart—just like them. They will be informed about new varieties and components of grief in our modern world and will be comforted by hearing the presence of God in new contexts that lead them to *live and move and have their being* in love that is stronger than death."

—**Dr. Fran Tilton Shelton**, Founder of Faith & Grief Ministries and author of *No Winter Lasts Forever: A Memoir of Loving Bob and Loathing Alzheimer's*

"Julie Yarbrough takes us on a thoughtful and sacred journey to the inner recesses of the most fundamental of human experiences—grief. Gently, she encourages the reader to release fear and examine grief's complexity as an individual and communal phenomenon. For those of us who have wept the bitter tears of loss, this book is a welcome balm to the soul."

—**Dr. Maria A. Dixon Hall**, Chief Diversity Officer and Senior Advisor to the President for Campus Cultural Intelligence Initiatives, Southern Methodist University

"Julie Yarbrough draws from her personal experiences and her deep Christian faith to offer an excellent resource for one who is living with grief. I commend it to clergy and counselors as they will find rich and helpful resources for their own vocations in working with people who are struggling with grief."

—**Bishop Michael McKee**, North Texas Conference of The United Methodist Church

"Julie's newest work is many things: wise, biblical, poetic. But, most of all, it's truly helpful. There are certain writers who radiate comfort. Julie is one of those. And Present Comfort could not be more timely."

–**Rev. Paul Rasmussen**, Senior Pastor, Highland Park
United Methodist Church

"In her new book, *Present Comfort: Meditations on Modern Loss and Grief*, author Julie Yarbrough beautifully and masterfully explores the human experience of loss and grief through the spiritual lens of Hope, Grace, and Peace. She invites us to connect with the spirit of who we are and who we were created to be, inviting us to know the everlasting love of those we grieve and that they will always be with us in spirit and love."

–**Rev. Caesar Rentie**, Vice President of Pastoral Services,
Methodist Health System of Dallas

PRESENT
COMFORT

PRESENT COMFORT

MEDITATIONS ON MODERN LOSS AND GRIEF

JULIE YARBROUGH

invite
PRESS

Plano, Texas

O God, in mystery and silence you are present in our lives, bringing new life out of destruction, hope out of despair, growth out of difficulty. We thank you that you do not leave us alone but labor to make us whole. Help us to perceive your unseen hand in the unfolding of our lives, and to attend to the gentle guidance of your Spirit, that we may know the joy you give your people.
Amen.[1]

CONTENTS

PART III—GOD PRESENT THROUGH US

PART IV—EMMANUEL: GOD PRESENT TO US

INTRODUCTION

When we pause from time to time to reflect on the events, occasions, and turning points that have formed and shaped us through the years, the faithful presence of God is the golden thread that weaves our life into its divine whole. And whether our perspective is one of clinical objectivity, emotional subjectivity, or one of an abandoned or tentative faith that has been shaken or stirred by the events of life beyond our control, when we take the panoramic view of where we have been and all that we have experienced over a lifetime, we discern with remarkable spiritual acuity that through every trial and triumph God is and was and shall forever be the invisible presence that is always with us, "Ever since the creation of the world his eternal power and divine nature, invisible though they are, have been understood and seen through the things he has made" (Romans 1:20).

A shocking succession of senseless acts of anger and aggression reflect the momentary social and spiritual imbalance in the world. It seems as if we are confronted with random acts of violence, school shootings, mass slayings, and natural disasters almost daily. Then suddenly our world is upended by a global pandemic that threatens the very fiber of our civilization. Unless we live apart from the mainstream of society, our lives are continuously affected by dire reports of tragedy and death.

As a society, we are forced to grieve more often and more publicly. At the same time, we grieve with an overwhelming desire for deep comfort. We find that comfort as we live into the presence of God, "My presence will go with you, and I will give you rest" (Exodus 33:14).

At this moment in time, in this day and age in which we live, our lived present has an urgency attributable in large part to the agitation, noise, and insistence of social media and a twenty-four-hour news cycle. To survive the daunting challenges unique to the twenty-first century, we must notice God's presence at work in the world. Perhaps more than ever, we desperately need a daily experience of the very real presence of God.

Within the Word of God, we discover much more than the transient comfort of the world, which can never fully satisfy the heartache of our inmost being. Rather we find the enduring comfort for which our soul yearns only in the sustaining presence of God. We are assured that God loves us, that God cares about us, that God walks alongside us in our grief, "Even though I walk through the valley of the shadow of death, I will fear no evil, for you are with me" (Psalm 23:4 ESV).

God is present to us—here and now—in the present. When we grieve, we ask, indeed we expect that God will be here now. Our need for God's presence inspires our most fervent prayers, "Do not cast me from your presence or take your Holy Spirit from me" (Psalm 51:11 NIV). God meets us where we are today, not at some later time. God is never distracted, delayed, or deterred. Because we are God's beloved children, we have God's complete, undivided attention. God is reliable. God is perfectly faithful. God is fully present to each one of us individually and personally, "But you have upheld me because of my integrity, and set me in your presence forever" (Psalm 41:12).

The presence of God is a gift to our lives, a gift of pure love that is unearned, unmerited, and undeserved, a present that fills our soul and makes us whole. When we receive a hand-crafted gift offered from the heart, we admire it, we appreciate it, we value the thought, time, and effort put into its creation and the love expressed in its giving. We are asked to do nothing more and nothing less than to receive the gift of God's presence with unending gratitude for the grace of the Giver, "From his fullness we have all received, grace upon grace" (John 1:16).

At times, our best expression of love is simply the gift of our presence. When one we love is grieving, often the only thing we have to offer is ourselves. In the very silence of being there, being present, wordlessly we express our care and support. And within our presence, there is the gift of God's presence, "For 'In him we live and move and have our being'" (Acts 17:28).

Present Comfort reflects on some of the more difficult grief issues of our day from the perspective of Scripture, including collective grief, collateral grief, survivor torment, outcast grief, unresolved grief, and reconciliation, to name a few. Perhaps one of the most complicated iterations of grief is triggered by the emotional fracture of suicide. Though *Present Comfort* offers many verses of Scripture and meditations that address aspects of personal trauma and tragedy, it does not specifically focus on the profoundly personal emotional and spiritual effect of suicide on those who survive. The book is intended to help identify and resolve many of the issues that may arise from the devastation of loss through the comfort and support of Scripture.

Like you, I have faced death in the first person. Although I am not a therapist or professional, I have immersed myself in understanding my life-changing encounter with grief since the death of my beloved husband. The hope is that *Present Comfort* will inspire spiritual insight and a deeper understanding of the presence of God to those who grieve and provide perspective for those who desire to share in the language and heart of grief. May each whisper of God's comfort be an assurance of the presence of God.

O LORD, you have searched me and known me.
You know when I sit down and when I rise up;
    you discern my thoughts from far away.
You search out my path and my lying down,
    and are acquainted with all my ways.
Even before a word is on my tongue,
    O LORD, you know it completely.
You hem me in, behind and before,
    and lay your hand upon me.
Such knowledge is too wonderful for me;
    it is so high that I cannot attain it.
Where can I go from your spirit?
    Or where can I flee from your presence?
If I ascend to heaven, you are there;
    if I make my bed in Sheol, you are there.
If I take the wings of the morning
    and settle at the farthest limits of the sea,
even there your hand shall lead me,
    and your right hand shall hold me fast.
If I say, "Surely the darkness shall cover me,
    and the light around me become night,"
even the darkness is not dark to you;
    the night is as bright as the day,
    for darkness is as light to you.
—Psalm 139:1-12

PART I

GOD PRESENT WITH US

UNISON GRIEF

For those around the world who are helpless onlookers to the destruction of a global pandemic or intentional acts of senseless violence, when life-altering events occur, our first impulse is to join hands and hearts across continents and the continuum of life to grieve in unison the death of each life lost to incomprehensible devastation. Whatever our faith conviction about the power and presence of God in the world, instinctively we reach within ourselves to pray individually and as one for the comfort of each person who survives and grieves.

As media saturation inevitably seeps into every crevice of the details, the word *mass* grabs our attention: mass infection, mass attack, mass destruction. And while *mass* may describe the scope of an event, there is a gaping emotional void when victims of unbridled contagion, personal and national terrorism, catastrophic weather events, and oppression of every kind are lumped together as part of an indeterminate *mass*.

Every person included as part of a media-described *mass* is a human being, whether alive or dead. When life ends because of an inexplicable *mass* occurrence of disease or disaster, we are painfully reminded that each individual has a unique story, "We spend our years as a tale that is told" (Psalm 90:9 KJV). Grief defies every assumption of *mass* because above all else, grief is individual and personal. When there is shared trauma, we are compelled to react and feel beyond the sweeping generalities of *mass* and grieve both individually and in unison the sacred loss of each human life.

We grieve as one when we hear a daughter describe the heartbreak of being able to do nothing more than look through a window because of restrictions imposed to prevent the spread of a viral infection, unable to be with her mother while she is dying alone. We hear a distraught mother say through the uncontrollable tears of a shattered heart, awash in disbelief and grief, "I don't know where my son is," only later to learn that he died in a mass shooting.

While it is impossible to ignore the tectonic social and moral change evident in life all around us—for better or for worse—with borderless illness and mass slayings there is a certain aggregate confusion that echoes the anger, frustration, and conflicted emotions of chaos. The psalmist David expressed his human fear, "For I hear the whispering of many—terror all around!—as they scheme together against me, as they plot to take my life" (Psalm 31:13).

We grieve as one when we consider the ripple effect of sudden, unexpected loss on those who survive—not only family members, but also friends, colleagues, neighbors, school friends, church communities, and on and on. For each individual who dies, there are hundreds, perhaps even thousands of people whose lives are unalterably changed by the cruel, untimely death of one they know and love. With renewed reverence for life and spiritual respect for the mystery of death, we grieve as one each living, breathing soul— each father, mother, child, son, daughter, wife, husband and every other relationship of spirit and bond that connects us one to another.

We grieve as one when we honor the meaning and value of each life made for a specific purpose in the divine order of creation, made in the image of a loving, caring God. As one we pray that God will comfort those who grieve, "both low and high, rich and poor together" (Psalm 49:2). We pray that God will give strength and courage to all those whose hearts are broken. We pray that the destructive power of a viral epidemic or willful brutality will be overcome through God's infinite goodness, mercy, and grace.

> Who will contend with me?
> Let us stand up together.
> Who are my adversaries?
> Let them confront me.
> It is the LORD GOD who helps me.

—Isaiah 50:8-9

We grieve together—in unison, as one—fortified by the comfort and strength of our faith to endure through the power and presence of God, "No testing has overtaken you that is not common to everyone. God is faithful, and he will not let you be tested beyond your strength, but with the testing he will also provide the way out so that you may be able to endure it" (1 Corinthians 10:13).

> In you, O LORD, I seek refuge;
>   do not let me ever be put to shame;
>   in your righteousness deliver me.
> Incline your ear to me;
>   rescue me speedily.
> Be a rock of refuge for me,
>   a strong fortress to save me.
> You are indeed my rock and my fortress;
>   for your name's sake lead me and guide me,

take me out of the net that is hidden for me,
for you are my refuge.
Into your hand I commit my spirit;
you have redeemed me, O LORD, faithful God.
You hate those who pay regard to worthless idols,
but I trust in the LORD.
I will exult and rejoice in your steadfast love,
because you have seen my affliction;
you have taken heed of my adversities,
and have not delivered me into the hand of the
enemy;
you have set my feet in a broad place.

Love the LORD, all you his saints.
The LORD preserves the faithful,
but abundantly repays the one who acts haughtily.
Be strong, and let your heart take courage,
all you who wait for the LORD.

—Psalm 31:1-8, 23-24

WHERE IS GOD?

When acts of random violence kill innocent people, wound and maim dozens of others, and bring an entire city to its knees, our heart is overwhelmed by the questions of large-scale grief, "Who did this?" "Why?" "How did this happen?" When an elusive virus erupts, causing a pandemic that holds the entire globe hostage, we want to know what caused it and how it could spread so quickly.

When people die violently, suddenly, or unexpectedly, the human heart is changed in ways unlike any other grief. The immediate shock of the moment co-exists with anger, outrage, and fear. A sense of helplessness seeps into every corner of our being and shakes the very foundation of our life and all that we hold dear. We insist on answers when there are none, we question and probe our faith, "If the LORD is with us, why then has all this happened to us?" (Judges 6:13). From the depths of our minds and hearts, we hear within our being the unspoken question, "Where is God?"

The assassination of President John F. Kennedy in Dallas on November 22, 1963 caused an outpouring of national grief that will forever be part of that city's humanity. Tourists still visit the grassy knoll to live into one of the singular moments that altered the history of the United States. When the infamous events of September 11, 2001 occurred in New York City, the question "Where is God?"

hung in the air like the thick smoke that overcame countless victims on that horrific day. Americans everywhere were momentarily paralyzed by shock and dark grief because of incomprehensible acts of terrorism perpetrated on a single day which forever changed lives across the nation, indeed across the world. The sights, the smells, and the palpable fear that permeated an ostensibly invincible city seemed to challenge every intimation of the presence of God.

After the bombings that targeted participants in the 2013 Boston marathon, one commentator remarked that Boston is a tough city that would survive and be stronger. Though cities rebuild and infrastructures recover, the grief of urban tragedy leaves an emotional blot on the community psyche and a scar that survives over many generations. Museums, monuments, fountains, gardens, and squares remind us of our loss and civic vulnerability to willful terrorism, even as they do the cathartic work of thoughtful remembrance. And though memorial structures do not answer the question "Where is God?", they remind those who visit and spend time there that each individual life is sacred.

Intellectually and spiritually we know that God does not cause violence. God does not visit us with disease, plagues, or pandemics. God does not plot against us, plan our harm, or punish us. Whatever our faith conviction, scripture assures us that the very nature of God is loving, kind, benevolent, compassionate, and merciful. When we suffer the pain of grief because of the human free will choices made by ourselves or others, we seek an outlet for our blame and indignation. If we pause to reflect and pray, we may direct our outrage and heartache toward God. Though God seldom provides us with an explanation for what has happened, we are never reproached for our outpouring of tangled emotions. Rather, through the power of God's presence, God moves us beyond the unanswerable "Why did this happen?" to the comfort and tentative hope of "How will I go on?". Though we may wrestle with our questions for a while, at last we are compelled by life to concede that we may never understand what happened. Our future lies in how we choose to go on. This is God at work in our lives—God present, God for us, especially when we suffer the trauma of unimaginable shock, loss, and grief, "He who rescued us from so deadly a peril will continue to rescue us; on him we have set our hope that he will rescue us again" (2 Corinthians 1:10).

Where is God? "My tears have been my food day and night, while people say to me continually, 'Where is your God?'" (Psalm 42:3). How do we know that God is present to us in the unalterable circumstances of life?

- God is in the outpouring of loving-kindness as strangers spontaneously reach out to help other strangers.

- God is in families suddenly brought closer together by a greater understanding of the gifts of life and love.

- God is in the strength and wisdom of leaders, first responders, professionals, and volunteers.

- God is at the heart of each act of worship when those who seek meaning in tragedy gather in community to call on the power and comfort of a loving, caring God.

- God is in all the anonymous acts of tender care that bear witness to the love of God for us all.

– God is in each moment of self-sacrifice, selflessness, and quiet heroism.

– God is in each whispered prayer for those whose grief is newer than ours.

– God is in life's worst tragedies when we are inspired to new heights of human goodness and compassion for others.

We find our power over evil, disease, destruction of life, and death in the presence of God.

> For the righteous will never be moved;
> they will be remembered forever.
> They are not afraid of evil tidings;
> their hearts are firm, secure in the LORD.
> Their hearts are steady, they will not be afraid;
> in the end they will look in triumph on their foes.

—Psalm 112:6-8

God is the strength within our grief, the victorious right hand that comforts us and guides us toward renewed hope, recovered love, and belief in the future, "Do not fear, for I am with you, do not be afraid, for I am your God; I will strengthen you, I will help you, I will uphold you with my victorious right hand" (Isaiah 41:10).

God is here, God is with us. In God's abiding presence we are comforted through the unlimited sufficiency of the grace of God, "Let us therefore approach the throne of grace with boldness, so that we may receive mercy and find grace to help in time of need" (Hebrews 4:16).

O love of God, how strong and true!
Eternal, and yet ever new;
Uncomprehended and unbought,
Beyond all knowledge and all thought.

O love of God, how deep and great!
Far deeper than man's deepest hate;
Self-fed, self-kindled, like the light,
Changeless, eternal, infinite.

O heavenly love, how precious still,
In days of weariness and ill!
In nights of pain and helplessness,
To heal, to comfort, and to bless.

O wide embracing, wondrous love,
We read thee in the sky above,
We read thee in the earth below,
In seas that swell, and streams that flow.

We read thee best in Him who came
To bear for us the cross of shame;
Sent by the Father from on high,
Our life to live, our death to die.

We read thy power to bless and save
Even in the darkness of the grave;
Still more in resurrection light,
We read the fullness of thy might.

O love of God, our shield and stay
Through all the perils of our way!
Eternal love, in thee we rest
Forever safe, forever blest.[2]

THE LOVE OF GRIEF

Grief is perhaps the most equal-opportunity experience in all of life. It is the great leveler of emotions, place, and time. At some age, at some time in life, everyone will know the sorrow and pain of grief. Grief is indifferent to our race, ethnicity, religion, or sexual orientation. We are not emotionally insulated from grief because of where we live, how educated we are, or how much money we have or do not have. Grief does not care whether we wear a business suit, a uniform, yoga pants, a T-shirt, or a clergy robe.

The most fundamental truth of grief is this: we grieve because we love. If we did not love, our hearts would not be broken by death. The greater our love, the deeper and more profound our grief.

- The love of grief is passionate—we cherish and memorialize those lost to us in death. We remember and never forget.

- The love of grief is compassionate—it reaches out, reconciles, restores, and builds up.

- The love of grief is infinite—amid the very worst of our grief, we glimpse the enormity of God's love and presence to us all.

– The love of grief is resilient—it is why we endure
the suffering of loss and persevere in hope. Despite
every evidence to the contrary, love never fails.

When we look into the depths of an international health
crisis, a planned assault on innocent human life, and each
instance of tragic, senseless death, we are compelled to consider questions about love that linger beyond the immediate
moment of shock and heartbreak. Would we forego the love
we shared with the one now lost to us in death simply to
avoid the pain of grief? No, surely we would not deny the
joy and glory of love only to avoid the possibility of loss—it
is simply unimaginable. If we take a step back for a moment,
we see in our grief perhaps the most heartfelt expression of
love beyond death. Grief comes from love. Grief springs
from love. Grief arises from a surrendered, selfless love. Grief
is the eternal connection of our love to the one now lost to
us in death.

Though it is not always so, we may find within the love
of grief our best response to life's worst tragedies. Without
fully understanding the *why*, we seek some redemptive value
so that death will not have been in vain. We harness our
grief-born love, first to change our own heart, then slowly
to change the world. And if not the whole world all at once,
we start where we are to be an influence for good, trusting
that one small swell of love shared with others will one day
become a sea change of spiritual outreach and compassion.

After the final words of comfort and encouragement are
spoken, the flowers wilt, and the last casserole is delivered
and consumed, what we discover is that grief never leaves us
where it finds us. We are forever changed by the experience
of death when it visits us individually and personally. Grief
may leave us disillusioned with life. Grief may leave us

angry, fearful, or even hate-filled. Or grief may leave us more convinced than ever of the goodness of life. As we experience violence, disease, and tragic death with ever-greater frequency in our current culture of self, grief may enable us to love others more deeply despite the certainty that evil is present in the world.

The inadequacy of our human resources inspires us to pray. We pray that God will overcome the power of evil in the world in which we live, "And lead us not into temptation, but deliver us from evil" (Matthew 6:13 RSV). We pray that we may be agents in the world of the comfort found only in the presence of God, "How precious is your steadfast love, O God! All people may take refuge in the shadow of your wings" (Psalm 36:7).

COLLECTIVE GRIEF

When an entire community is stunned by tragedy, a kind of collective grief envelops everyone, whether or not their life is touched directly by loss. Often this grief is more intense in small communities where there are few degrees of separation among neighbors, friends, and family. People know one another, many from birth, and are related by generations of ancestors committed to a shared geographic or religious heritage.

After one local tragedy in which a church building was seriously damaged, a reporter showed members of the congregation worshiping on Sunday in an open field. In the bright sunshine of a beautiful spring day, life's extremes and dreams collided as those gathered shared their collective and individual grief. Amid the public and private outpouring of love and care, there were tears. There was sadness. There was determination. There was hope, "And now, O Lord, what do I wait for? My hope is in you" (Psalm 39:7). And there was joy simply to be alive, connected heart to heart in the sacred bond of community.

The nature of collective grief is that sometimes it lifts rather quickly. When those believed to be responsible for senseless acts of terrorism are apprehended or identified, there is a sense of relief for those whose lives have been singularly focused on the fear and tension caused by the unknown. When grief blankets an entire community, the rites and rituals of collective grief comfort and reassure for the moment.

Yet long after the solemn occasions of public remembrance are over and a community resumes the rhythm of life in the mainstream, those whose loved ones have died grieve on. There will always be lingering collective grief in Newtown, Connecticut for the children and dedicated professionals capriciously slain on a tragic day in December 2012. It could not be otherwise. Those who survive live with chronic pain, deep, personal heartache, and endless conjecture about a future that will never be—the *what if* and *if only* at the core of the great, unanswered *why*.

Grief insists that we fully acknowledge what we are feeling about the death of one we love. It is a solitary faith journey of self-discovery that can be shared with a community, such as a grief support group, yet the true essence of grief is experienced individually within the solitude and silence of the soul and spirit. When we grieve, we cannot hide from ourselves within the safety of a community. We must confront our loss and pain at that deep place of personal frailty where we examine our heart, wrestle with our doubts, and grow into a richer, fuller faith. Ultimately, it is our faith that leads us away from grief toward emotional recovery and spiritual wholeness.

> Hear my prayer, O Lord;
> let my cry come to you.
> Do not hide your face from me
> in the day of my distress.
> Incline your ear to me;
> answer me speedily in the day when I call.

He has broken my strength in midcourse;
he has shortened my days.
"O my God," I say, "do not take me away
at the midpoint of my life,
you whose years endure
throughout all generations."
Long ago you laid the foundation of the earth,
and the heavens are the work of your hands.
They will perish, but you endure;
they will all wear out like a garment.
You change them like clothing, and they pass away;
but you are the same, and your years have no end.
The children of your servants shall live secure;
their offspring shall be established in your presence"
—Psalm 102:1-2, 23-28

In the presence of God we find the comfort that sustains us when the loss and pain of collective grief seem almost unbearable. On the last occasion my beloved husband was in the pulpit, he offered this pastoral prayer, "We have come this far by faith, and we will continue to walk with our hand in yours wherever you lead us." Within this spiritual affirmation we find the promise of faith that in life, in death, in life beyond death—and in our grief—God is with us. We are not alone.

POURED LOVE

At a Maundy Thursday service one year, I listened to a meditation on the mandate of the new commandment, "I give you a new commandment, that you love one another. Just as I have loved you, you also should love one another" (John 13:34). The love of the new commandment was illustrated through the ancient ritual of foot washing as a symbolic stream of water was poured from a pitcher into a basin, "Then he poured water into a basin and began to wash the disciples' feet and to wipe them with the towel that was tied around him" (John 13:5). In an exquisite moment of spiritual grace, I heard the sound of poured love.

The apostle Paul writes this about how we grow through the tests and trials of life, "...knowing that suffering produces endurance, and endurance produces character, and character produces hope, and hope does not disappoint us, because God's love has been poured into our hearts through the Holy Spirit that has been given us" (Romans 5:3-5). The uniquely personal experience of the death of one we love inevitably moves us through this logical emotional and spiritual sequence when we grieve. As we advance from suffering to endurance, we are reminded that God's perfect plan is constantly at work in our lives.

The measure of endurance and character we acquire because of our experience of suffering and grief should lead us inevitably to reclaim hope as the highest and best evidence of our faith, "Now faith is the assurance of things hoped for, the conviction of things not seen" (Hebrews 11:1). We are assured that hope does not disappoint us because God's love has been poured into our hearts—not trickled in or carefully measured and added in by the cupful, but poured in without limitation. Our hearts are filled to capacity, sometimes to overflowing, by hope, a hope that does not disappoint us because God's love has been poured into our hearts through the gift of the Holy Spirit, "But the Advocate, the Holy Spirit, whom the Father will send in my name, will teach you everything, and remind you of all that I have said to you" (John 14:26).

When we grieve, hope may seem elusive. If we feel that all is lost, hope seems to require more effort than we are able to summon, "Now hope that is seen is not hope. For who hopes for what is seen?" (Romans 8:24). It takes spiritual energy, patience, and steadfast endurance to persevere in hope, "But if we hope for what we do not see, we wait for it with patience" (Romans 8:25). We may question whether we should reinvest in life if there is a chance our hope will again be disappointed.

Why are you cast down, O my soul,
and why are you disquieted within me?
Hope in God; for I shall again praise him,
my help and my God
—Psalm 42:11

We dare to hope again in life because we are filled by the dynamic, liquid power of God's poured out love, "For you, O Lord, are my hope, my trust, O LORD, from my youth" (Psalm 71:5). When we grieve, we express our faith as hope rather than hopelessness. If we live hopefully rather than in despair, we affirm that we are people of hope because God's love has been poured into our hearts, "Let your steadfast love, O LORD, be upon us, even as we hope in you" (Psalm 33:22). In truth, grief can be the most honest and faithful place we will ever stand to find the true meaning of hope when we are face-to-face with the emotional surrender of grief, "Rejoice in hope, be patient in suffering, persevere in prayer" (Romans 12:12).

If we attune our heart and listen carefully, we can hear the steady stream of poured out love as we experience the power and comfort of the presence of God, "so that times of refreshing may come from the presence of the Lord" (Acts 3:20). Our soul is refreshed when the steadfast love and faithfulness of God pour into our heart with the hope that restores our spirit to wonder and gratitude for the sacred gift of life.

As those who live in hope, we are blessed with a faith that is richer and deeper because we have survived the death of one we love. The poured love that fills our heart with hope is the very essence of the presence of God.

> But this I call to mind,
> and therefore I have hope:
> The steadfast love of the LORD never ceases,
> his mercies never come to an end;
> they are new every morning;
> great is your faithfulness.
>
> —Lamentations 3:21-23

COLLATERAL GRIEF

I n our present-day society we are confronted with acts of
violence that are simply unimaginable. If we scrutinize
photos and videos of survivors, friends, colleagues, and
loved ones, we see in their faces the unspeakable pain and
sorrow of intense, personal grief. The picture of a desperate,
heartbroken mother with the cross of Ash Wednesday still
freshly signed on her forehead told the story of destruction
and despair that devastated the community of Parkland,
Florida on a holy day of remembrance, "We are hard pressed
on every side, but not crushed; perplexed, but not in despair;
persecuted, but not abandoned; struck down, but not
destroyed" (2 Corinthians 4:8-9 NIV).

If we read beyond the headlines, we realize that hundreds,
perhaps even thousands of people are exponentially affected
by both catastrophic injuries and the untimely death of those
they know and love. As witnesses to events that embody the
force of evil at work in the world, we may be surprised by
the delayed reaction of our emotions. We grope for what it is
we should be feeling as shock, disbelief, and anger erupt and
bubble to the surface. At the far reach of our bewilderment
we seek to grasp the motivation of the perpetrator as we try
to understand and make sense of the senseless.

Collateral grief is our most fundamental response to the
pain and suffering of others, which we express as heartfelt

compassion. When a series of dire events occur in rapid succession they vie for our emotional attention. If there has not been sufficient time or space to restore some sense of emotional equilibrium, our compassion easily ricochets from one tragedy to the next, fueled by exuberant media coverage and the extremes of geography, place, and time. We feel oddly splintered, emotionally fragmented in our ability to focus. We respond with frantic spiritual energy that leaves us exhausted in the aftermath of each tragic occurrence. This is sometimes described as compassion fatigue. The truth of our humanity is that we are limited in our ability to live into the grief of an entire community at times of sustained crisis unless we are in some way personally affected.

The sad commentary of recent decades is that random acts of violence seem to occur with almost clockwork regularity. Twenty-six living, breathing people were killed in a matter of seconds as a church in a small community met for worship on a Sunday morning. Innocent, unsuspecting victims were capriciously killed at a movie theater in Colorado, at a nightclub in Florida, at a superstore in Texas, and at concerts in Las Vegas, Manchester, England, and Paris, France. Terrorist truck drivers set on intentional mayhem targeted anyone in their path on a bridge in London, England, and near a beach in Nice, France. We are at once outraged and impotent to deter those who would willfully inflict bodily injury in the name of righteousness, hatred, or a twisted, sociopathic disregard for the sacredness of life.

Collateral grief extends to every circumstance of life that calls forth our human compassion. Within a very compressed period of time, we hear of simultaneous natural disasters—tsunamis, floods, tornadoes—that end in slow recovery, sometimes against insurmountable odds, which may lead to a demographic shift within an entire area or neighborhood. Earthquakes in Mexico quickly followed by earthquakes in the Middle East killed hundreds of men, women, and children, each a beloved child of God. Relentless hurricanes devastated a major city and the livelihood of an entire island nation within a matter of hours. Time and again wildfires aggressively pursue an arbitrary path of destruction that leave thousands of people homeless and the most helpless dead.

Not long after the 2017 shootings in Sutherland Springs, Texas, a perplexed acquaintance tossed this question into the universe, "How am I supposed to understand the incomprehensible death of so many innocent victims?" This expression of spiritual confusion well describes how many of us react to the range of complex emotions that at once confound our sensibilities and demand our collateral grief.

The answer is that God has not endowed us with the ability to understand death. Rather, God created us to empathize with other human beings with an outpouring of love and compassion. Though we may draw conclusions from what we observe or read, generally God does not provide us with logical understanding or insight into the *why* of random violence, terrorism, and natural disasters. Beyond some insight into the possible reason or motivation for each bad act or event, usually we are not offered an explanation, a rationale, or access to the mysteries that God alone fully comprehends.

Whom have I in heaven but you?
And there is nothing on earth that I desire other than you.
My flesh and my heart may fail,
but God is the strength of my heart and my portion forever.

—Psalm 73:25-26

The limitations of our understanding urge us to the edge of our capacity for compassion—the unconditional, boundless gift of love that is ours to lavish on those whose lives are devastated by incidents and circumstances beyond our human understanding, "according to the riches of his grace that he lavished on us" (Ephesians 1:7-8).

The compassion of collateral grief lived out as kindness, care, and love is the highest and best expression of our solidarity with others. God's comfort and continuous care for each child of God's own creation knows no limits. Beyond our acceptance of God's infinite mysteries, the assurance of our faith both in life and in death is the certainty of the presence of God, "Nevertheless, I am continually with you; you hold my right hand" (Psalm 73:23).

SHEER SILENCE

He said, "Go out and stand on the mountain before
the Lord, for the Lord is about to pass by." Now
there was a great wind, so strong that it was split-
ting mountains and breaking rocks in pieces before
the Lord, but the Lord was not in the wind; and
after the wind an earthquake, but the Lord was not
in the earthquake; and after the earthquake a fire,
but the Lord was not in the fire; and after the fire
a sound of sheer silence. When Elijah heard it, he
wrapped his face in his mantle and went out and
stood at the entrance of the cave. Then there came
a voice to him that said, "What are you doing here,
Elijah?"
—1 Kings 19:11-13

Only seldom, if ever, are we given instructions on where
and when we might expect to hear directly from
God. Though we may pray fervently, more often than not
we have little expectation that God will speak directly and
unmistakably to us, especially when our soul is stifled by the
heartache of grief.

In the aftermath of some stunning triumphs and a
dramatic turn of events, Elijah flees from the wrath of
Jezebel and runs for his life. When he leaves, he goes on a
kind of personal pilgrimage, first to the wilderness, then to
Mount Horeb where he seeks safety and protection in a cave.

There God speaks to Elijah and instructs him on what to do and what he can expect to happen. Specifically, Elijah is instructed to go outside the cave and stand on the mountain because God is about to pass by. Obediently, Elijah goes to the appointed place. Yet before he experiences the presence of God, he is subjected to a noisy, spectacular display of extreme weather events that prove beyond all doubt that God is in neither the wind, nor the earthquake, nor the fire.

Rather, the presence of God is revealed to Elijah in a way that is completely unexpected—through "a sound of sheer silence." The absolute presence of God was not *in* the sound of sheer silence; the absolute presence of God *was* the sound of sheer silence. Elijah is overpowered. When he realizes that he is in the presence of God, he covers his face, withdraws in humility, and stands at the entrance of the cave.

We live in a world of noise and distraction in which we teeter precariously between real-life experience and technology overload. Many spend more time taking photos of the world than actually seeing the world. Because we are conditioned to be uncomfortable with silence, we tend to fill the void with sound and words. News commentators, politicians, activists, opinion makers, influencers, and a host of loud voices on social media compete to saturate us with the rhetoric of self-interest. Those who describe themselves as extroverts may feel anxious when there is absolute quiet, while those who self-identify as introverts seem to thrive on silence. A periodic absence of noise is essential for our emotional, mental, and spiritual recovery from experiences of trauma, tragedy, and grief. To recognize and access the presence of God within the beauty of sheer silence, we must first distance ourselves from the cacophony of worldly noise.

A parallel interpretation of "a sound of sheer silence" is God present to us as a "still small voice" (1 Kings 19:12

KJV). When God speaks to us, even in a still small voice, we expect as Elijah did to hear understandable words and specific directions. Yet God's words to us are not always purely instructive or spoken in simple declarative sentences such as "do this" or "do not do that." Before we can hear God speak, we must quiet our inmost being, wait, and listen with expectation for the voice of God to speak both through sound and in silence, "Be still before the LORD, and wait patiently for him" (Psalm 37:7). The power of sheer silence continually invites us into the presence of God. There alone can we "Be still, and know that I am God!" (Psalm 46:10).

Our greatest challenge comes when God speaks to us in questions. After Elijah fled from Jezebel, he went first into the wilderness. Awash in self-pity, he sat down under a juniper tree and asked God to let him die. God spoke to Elijah and asked, "What are you doing here?" Elijah's answer was defensive—he cited the reasons he felt so defeated and despondent. God then commanded Elijah to go from the wilderness to the mountain.

God may use our response to God's questions as a catalyst to direct us to a different place in life. On the mountain, Elijah experienced the presence of God in "a sound of sheer silence." Overwhelmed, Elijah retreated to his place of physical safety, where God asked again, "What are you doing here?" When Elijah gave the exact same reply as he did in the wilderness, God disallowed his excuses and told him what he must do. Elijah was a man who heard God and used his experience of the presence of God to serve God throughout his life of prophetic witness. The question "What are you doing here?" bears repeating in our own lives as we move through the experience of grief.

When we grieve, like Elijah we may feel tone deaf, stuck in a place of hopelessness. As we react to the death of one we love, we may try to reinvent ourselves, though we do not always achieve the desired outcome. If we compromise any part of that which is the spiritual foundation of our soul and inmost being, like Elijah we may have no good answer or even the will to respond when God asks, "What are you doing here?" Yet one day we realize that our experience of grief has been fully capitalized and we are richer, better, and stronger spiritually for having mourned the death of one we love. In that sacred moment, we experience the wordless embodiment of divine presence, the sound of sheer silence that mutes the atonal noise of the world and gently quiets even the music of the spheres. In the perfect reverence of sheer silence we encounter the presence of God, "If the LORD had not been my help, my soul would soon have lived in the land of silence" (Psalm 94:17).

HIDDEN
IN PLAIN SIGHT

Sometimes a new perspective on a single word or idea can penetrate our uneven grief emotions and get our attention in an unexpected way. It is the light bulb effect, the "aha" moment when we at last understand some deeper truth that gives us unexpected insight into the nature of God. When this happens, we are strengthened and inspired to move forward in our grief.

The psalmists paint some particularly vivid word pictures, often framed in praise and thanksgiving to God. When we grieve, it may be difficult to feel grateful because it seems as though our entire world lies in ruins around us. Most would probably agree, there is precious little that seems praiseworthy about death when one we love is no longer with us in this life. Yet the fact that we survive and that God empowers us to grow into our changed life are sufficient reasons to offer our unreserved gratitude to God. It is a sacred responsibility of grief to be grateful for the gift of life, even in the face of loss and sorrow.

> Blessed be the LORD,
> for he has wondrously shown his steadfast love to me
> when I was beset as a city under siege.
> I had said in my alarm,

"I am driven far from your sight."
But you heard my supplications
when I cried out to you for help.

—Psalm 31:21-22

If you follow media outlets that focus on world news, probably you have some impression of what a city under siege looks like. Usually the scene is utter chaos and complete mayhem. No less besieged and beset is a world invaded by a viral pandemic. Though with illness there may be little visible evidence of large-scale destruction, the toll in human life is more devastating and significant than the loss of anything man-made or material.

When we grieve, for a while our life may seem like a city under siege. Our world is turned both upside down and inside out by the death of one we love. We are confronted at every turn, beset by the forces of change. Rebuilding a city that is damaged or destroyed may progress over several generations. In contrast, some will never recover from the trauma and permanent loss of a century-event health crisis. When we grieve, it is impossible to make quick order out of the destruction in our lives after the death of one we love.

At the core of our grief, the presence of God is hidden in plain sight within each gesture of grace that comforts our heart. God's love defends our life. God's love enfolds us in everlasting arms. God's love assures us that God cares for us individually and personally, especially when we grieve. Though God is invisible, God's love is visible all around us if we will but lift up our head and heart to experience every small and large manifestation of the comfort and presence of God.

When we grieve, we may feel isolated from everyone and everything. We may feel alienated from God, "driven far from your sight." Though it may be alarming to find ourselves in this unfamiliar place of heart and soul, God is never threatened by our emotions, especially the outpouring of a grief-stricken heart. God is trustworthy. God is infinitely patient. God understands our grief.

I waited patiently for the LORD;
he inclined to me and heard my cry.
He drew me up from the desolate pit,
out of the miry bog,
and set my feet upon a rock,
making my steps secure.
He put a new song in my mouth,
a song of praise to our God.
Many will see and fear,
and put their trust in the LORD.

—Psalm 40:1-3

We want help, we need help, but can we rely on the presence of God in our grief? Our assurance is that God hears and answers our prayers when we cry to God for help, "Whatever you ask for in prayer with faith, you will receive" (Matthew 21:22). We express our faith in God through prayer, even when there are no words other than, "Lord, help me" (Matthew 15:25).

On a walk through the neighborhood one afternoon, I saw a little girl tangled in her bicycle. In a small, anxious voice she cried out in fearful distress. "Help me," she said. I crossed the street, murmured a few words of comfort, then pointed her toward her nearby home. Like this small child, God untangles our lives, comforts us in our grief, and guides us on our way to spiritual safety and home.

Though we suffer for a while, we are never driven from God's sight. Rather, we are heartened because of the assurance that the presence of God is with us everywhere, at all times, forever, "Take heart, it is I; do not be afraid" (Matthew 14:27). We give thanks continually for the steadfast love and presence of God, hidden in plain sight.

No need to panic over alarms or surprises,
or predictions that doomsday's just around the corner,
Because GOD will be right there with you;
he'll keep you safe and sound.

—Proverbs 3:25-26 MSG

NO FEAR IN LOVE

Love and fear share a kind of polar opposite kinship. When we grieve, most of us experience the kind of fear that has little to do with love. Some of us live with a kind of chronic fear that feels like quiet desperation. Some of us live with low-grade fear that causes us to be constantly on the defensive. Though some of us live through grief with a fair amount of equanimity, from time to time we may be unexpectedly waylaid by episodes of fear that threaten to unhinge us completely. Grief, fear, love—strange bedfellows indeed.

In grief there is a precarious balance between love and fear. When death upends our world, nothing is the same—everything changes. Suddenly the emotional and spiritual imbalance of grief sparks our worst fears. Fear is compounded by countless, sometimes nameless questions—for some there will be answers, for others not. In grief, fear thrives on the underside of the unknown.

The dilemma of grief is whether we succumb to our fears and live in darkness or find the perfect love that casts out fear within the comfort and presence of God, "There is no fear in love, but perfect love casts out fear; for fear has to do with punishment, and whoever fears has not reached perfection in love" (1 John 4:18). This is the faith part of grief—the seeking, stretching, striving part that makes us better as we pursue the hope and joy of fearless love. Our ongoing quest for perfection in love inspires us to persevere in life despite the absence of the one we love and now grieve.

In darker moments of pain and sorrow, some may feel that the death of a loved one is punishment. For a long time after my beloved husband died, I had a very real sense that I was being punished. I grew up in a home ruled by fear and punishment and was well schooled in the consequences of imperfect love. It took many months of deep soul searching before I could fully embrace the biblical truth that God does not punish us, that illness, accidents, and death are not personal. God is, in fact, the one true embodiment of perfect love.

When fear and love coexist in a relationship, many who grieve are emotionally conflicted after the death of one they love. Deconstructing the walls we carefully erect as protection from our fear of punishment is arduous work which sometimes requires the perspective of a counselor or therapist. If we assess the damage to our heart and soul and rely on the resources of our faith for healing and wholeness, in time we are able to open ourselves to a different kind of love that is more perfect and courageous than we have ever before known.

Perfect love casts out fear. If you have ever had a child or held a child, or if you are grieving the death of an infant or a child, you know firsthand that children are not born with fear. You have felt the sweet breath of God's perfect love in the unconditional love of an innocent child that trusts completely without so much as a whisper of fear. This is about as close to perfect love as any of us will ever experience on this side of heaven. This is the love of God, the fearless love with which we are born, the perfect love that speaks heart to heart and binds our soul together forever with those we love and grieve, "And now faith, hope, and love abide, these three; and the greatest of these is love" (1 Corinthians 13:13).

We are not intended to live in fear or in the shadow of fear left over from the past. As we sort out our relationships and reconnect with our spiritual and emotional center, over time we realize that fear is not where we will find our future. Rather, we are created to live in the presence of God with the perfect love that comforts us in our grief, assures us of life after death, and casts out every fear. We are to "go on toward perfection" (Hebrews 6:1).

THE FAITH
OF GRIEF

The hardscrabble faith of grief is altogether different from an unbruised faith that has not been tried and tested by a firsthand experience of death, life's most certain inevitability. If our world has been inverted by the death of one we love, for a while our faith may seem muddled as we ask hard questions that test the truth of what we say we believe.

When one we love dies, the raw fear that easily overwhelms our heart and spirit has little to do with the faith of grief. Our spiritual fortitude and forbearance are challenged by a fear that immobilizes us in the present, a fear that panics us about the future, a fear that threatens our emotional equilibrium, a fear that makes us teeter on the edge of despair, a fear that delights in our desperation. Whatever our grief-driven response to fear, in and of itself, fear has little to do with the conviction of our faith.

The faith of grief excels in perseverance. In the face of fear and the emotional turmoil of grief, like the apostle Paul we tie a knot and hang on, "forgetting what lies behind and straining forward to what lies ahead, I press on toward the goal for the prize of the heavenly call of God in Christ Jesus" (Philippians 3:13-14). When we grieve, every breath we take is an expression of our faith. We persevere until life moves forward into the future, "for we walk by faith, not by sight" (2 Corinthians 5:7).

We measure the faith of grief by who we are becoming. Because of our experience of grief, we feel stronger and more capable, fortified for the rest of our life. As the cycle of grief slowly comes to an end, we see more clearly who we are and where we have been. The faith of grief brings us full circle to a place of new beginning on the other side of grief, "think of the various tests you encounter as occasions for joy. After all, you know that the testing of your faith produces endurance. Let this endurance complete its work so that you may be fully mature, complete, and lacking in nothing" (James 1:2-4 CEB). The faith of grief is mature and complete, lacking in nothing.

The experience of David is a paradigm for the faith of grief.

> The LORD struck the child that Uriah's wife bore
> to David, and it became very ill. David therefore
> pleaded with God for the child; David fasted, and
> went in and lay all night on the ground. The elders
> of his house stood beside him, urging him to rise
> from the ground; but he would not, nor did he eat
> food with them.
> On the seventh day the child died. And the servants
> of David were afraid to tell him that the child was
> dead; for they said, "While the child was still alive,
> we spoke to him, and he did not listen to us; how
> then can we tell him the child is dead? He may do
> himself some harm."
> But when David saw that his servants were whispering
> together, he perceived that the child was dead; and
> David said to his servants, "Is the child dead?"
> They said, "He is dead."

Then David rose from the ground, washed,
anointed himself, and changed his clothes. He went
into the house of the LORD, and worshiped; he then
went to his own house; and when he asked, they set
food before him and he ate.
Then his servants said to him, "What is this thing
that you have done? You fasted and wept for the
child while it was alive; but when the child died,
you rose and ate food."
He said, "While the child was still alive, I fasted
and wept; for I said, 'Who knows? The LORD may
be gracious to me, and the child may live.' But
now he is dead; why should I fast? Can I bring him
back again? I shall go to him, but he will not return to
me."

—2 Samuel 12:15-23

Though our heart will always remember the one we love
and now grieve, gradually the experience of death becomes
part of the background of our life. When grief is no longer at
the forefront of our every thought and we are at last focused
more on the here and now than on the past, we find that
our faith has a different mettle. We have a deeper spiritual
connection to God. We know with certainty that through
the presence of God, faith redeems our broken heart to new
life.

Love and faithfulness meet together;
righteousness and peace kiss each other.
Faithfulness springs forth from the earth,
and righteousness looks down from heaven.

—Psalm 85:10-11 NIV

PERFECT
FAITHFULNESS

When we experience the death of one we love, we may feel compelled to conform our emotions to some prescribed expectation of what we should feel or how we should act to express the sadness and sorrow of our grief. In truth, there is no perfect way to grieve. Grief is messy—it is not for perfectionists.

Faithfulness is perhaps the very essence of a true marriage. We honor our spouse with the gift of unreserved trust, the fidelity of our spirit, and the loyalty of our heart. Do we do this perfectly over a lifetime together? No, surely not. We speak a disloyal word, we demand our own way, we insist that our understanding of relationship is the preferred ideal. Despite our human imperfections, when we work at perfect faithfulness in a healthy, growing relationship, we stand a good chance of getting it right most of the time.

Belief in the perfect faithfulness of God is our best hope for surviving the death of one we love, "Let us hold fast to the confession of our hope without wavering, for he who has promised is faithful" (Hebrews 10:23). God is faithful, God is perfect, God is a promise keeper.

The Rock, his work is perfect;
for all his ways are justice.
A God of faithfulness and without iniquity,
just and right is he.

—Deuteronomy 32:4 RSV

God's perfect faithfulness has been my comfort through
every personal experience of grief. I know with certainty
that God has never once let go of my hand, not even for an
instant. I know with certainty that God has walked beside
me every step of the way through the sorrow and pain of
profound grief. The way through our heartbreak and grief
is found in the perfect faithfulness of the presence of God,
expressed with heartfelt conviction in the assurance of the
psalms.

- "For the word of the LORD is upright, and all his
  work is done in faithfulness" (Psalm 33:4).

- "Your steadfast love, O LORD, extends to the heavens, your faithfulness to the clouds" (Psalm 36:5).

- "Do not, O LORD, withhold your mercy from me;
  let your steadfast love and your faithfulness keep
  me safe forever" (Psalm 40:11).

- "For your steadfast love is as high as the heavens;
  your faithfulness extends to the clouds" (Psalm
  57:10).

- "I will sing of your steadfast love, O LORD, forever; with my mouth I will proclaim your faithfulness to all generations" (Psalm 89:1).

– "I declare that your steadfast love is established forever; your faithfulness is as firm as the heavens" (Psalm 89:2).

– "For the Lord is good; his steadfast love endures forever, and his faithfulness to all generations" (Psalm 100:5).

– "For your steadfast love is higher than the heavens, and your faithfulness reaches to the clouds" (Psalm 108:4).

– "Hear my prayer, O Lord; give ear to my supplications in your faithfulness; answer me in your righteousness" (Psalm 143:1).

Our comfort and hope are secure in the steadfast love of the presence of God. In life, in death, in life beyond death, God is perfectly faithful.

Lord, you are my God;
I will exalt you and praise your name,
for in perfect faithfulness
you have done wonderful things,
things planned long ago.

—Isaiah 25:1 NIV

God Knows[3]

And I said to the man who stood at the gate of the year:
"Give me a light that I may tread safely into the unknown."
And he replied:
"Go out into the darkness and put your hand into the Hand of God.

That shall be to you better than light and safer than
a known way."
So I went forth, and finding the Hand of God, trod
gladly into the night.
And He led me towards the hills and the breaking
of day in the lone East.
So heart be still:
What need our little life
Our human life to know,
If God hath comprehension?
In all the dizzy strife
Of things both high and low,
God hideth His intention.
God knows. His will
Is best. The stretch of years
Which wind ahead, so dim
To our imperfect vision,
Are clear to God. Our fears
Are premature; In Him,
All time hath full provision.
Then rest: until
God moves to lift the veil
From our impatient eyes,
When, as the sweeter features
Of Life's stern face we hail,
Fair beyond all surmise
God's thought around His creatures
Our mind shall fill.

OUTCAST GRIEF

When our lives are torn apart by acts of intentional, seemingly random violence, seldom do we venture beyond the shock of our own grief to consider the silent exile of those who know and love the perpetrator. Rarely do we pause to consider how the lives of those who are marginalized by the bad acts of others are irrevocably affected.

The widow of an angry husband who shot and wounded a congressman and four others at a baseball practice in Washington, DC said that she lives with daily torment over what more she might have done to help her spouse, "'I get up every morning feeling guilty because I didn't stop it. . . I wake up with hot sweats, thinking: You should have known. You should have known.' Neighbors urged her not to mow the lawn, for fear she might be attacked. A friend dispersed her trash around town to avoid snoops. A stranger once walked up to her at a grocery store and slapped her across the face. She cried all the way home."[4]

Parents of the seventeen-year-old adolescent who killed eight students and two teachers and wounded thirteen others at a high school in Santa Fe, Texas said they were "mostly in the dark" about the motive behind the attack. They said that their son's actions were "incompatible with the boy we love. We are as shocked and confused as anyone else by these events…We share the public's hunger for answers."[5]

For each person whose life is permanently scarred as a victim of someone intent on willful harm, there are others who are rejected by society at large and live in shame as pariahs because of their relationship to the perpetrator.

- Parents who live alongside a child who withdraws into a life of secrecy are often dumbfounded when their child is identified as the "doer." Somehow, they have missed or ignored subtle cues of isolation and anger. Perhaps they have failed to sense the seething pain of a child who feels like a misfit, or one who has been the victim of bullying. Or they have not exercised their prerogative as a parent to access their child's computer, either fearful of a confrontation or unprepared for what they might discover in the dark world of the internet. When weapons are available and easily accessible within the home, the potential for regret is part of the calculated risk of responsibility for parents.

- A certain defiant righteousness permeates each act of extremism or terrorism when perpetrated by a group that represents a cause. After the deed is done, victory may be declared in the name of someone or something without regard for legal or moral consequences. With complete indifference to the sanctity of life, a kind of heartless self-justification defies the large-scale grief caused by violence. Family and friends separated by distance from those who rampage without regard for those who are killed, injured, or maimed for life usually react with horror, disbelief, and embarrassment.

For those who live with alienation, guilt, and remorse for the deeds of another, several universal qualities characterize their inverted experience of grief:

- a sense of personal failure because signs of a deeply troubled spirit were not clearly evident;

- a sense of personal accountability driven by an overwhelming impulse to atone for the sociopathic behavior of another;

- a sense of being ostracized, forced to live apart from the mainstream of life;

- a sense of unrelieved humiliation, heightened by the condemnation of others.

For those whose lives have been irreparably altered by the tragic, sudden, unexpected death of one they love, it is a formidable test of faith and spiritual substance to empathize with the woundedness of those who live with survivor torment. In our world, there is great need for universal forgiveness and mercy toward each person who bears the weight of blame on behalf of those who commit acts of human destruction.

Those who live in the purgatory of outcast grief are redeemed to life when we offer absolution, compassion, and the unconditional grace we find far beyond the bounds of mere spiritual discipline. The presence of God elevates our soul to a higher place that bears witness to the divine when we extend our heart freely to those who live with outcast grief, "Finally, all of you, have unity of spirit, sympathy, love for one another, a tender heart, and a humble mind. Do not repay evil for evil or abuse for abuse; but, on the contrary, repay with a blessing. It is for this that you were called—that you might inherit a blessing" (1 Peter 3:8-9).

SURVIVOR
TORMENT

Guilt is one of the most sinister emotions of grief. It is the tenacious self-reproach that sometimes surfaces when one we love dies. Most of us hang onto guilt like a dog with a bone. Like any high-octane fuel, guilt has the power to spark within us a raging bonfire of grief.

At its most fundamental, guilt is the feeling of responsibility or remorse for something real or imagined for which we hold ourselves accountable. After my husband died, I was plagued by an overwhelming sense of guilt. For many months I waged a fierce war within myself because I felt that I had failed in my self-appointed mission to restore him to good health. In the end, the sheer force of my love and determination could not conquer cancer or save his life. I felt that I had failed, yet in truth I had not. I was merely human and had no power over life and death.

Though my guilt was entirely irrational, it took many months to understand that I was no match for an unconquerable enemy, and accept that I had done nothing to cause my husband's illness or death. Slowly, over time, I shed my load of guilt like a too-heavy winter coat and eased into a life that felt lighter, my pockets filled with self-forgiveness and greater self-knowledge.

When we grieve, we may be overcome with guilt about what we did or did not do, or what we did or did not say—the "should haves" and "if onlys" that can stay with us for a long time. Slowly we realize that nothing is gained by continuing to rehearse words we will never be able to take back, or those we will never be able to speak to the one now lost to us in death.

Second-guessing ourselves prolongs our struggle with the guilt sometimes associated with unresolved emotions in relationship, especially in the aftermath of a protracted illness or sudden, traumatic death. We may feel remorse that we did not do enough or that we should have tried harder. We may experience an acute sense of failure if we believe that it was our personal responsibility to be an agent of rescue, "If only I had done (fill in the blank) differently." When we realize that nothing can be gained by holding on to that which we can never change, gradually we disengage from that which is counterproductive to our emotional recovery from the death of one we love, and unproductive for our experience of grief. Over time we are able to release most of the guilt that can easily distort a heartfelt experience of grief.

Survivor guilt is a common reaction if our life is spared when tragedy strikes those near us. We may feel as though we have done something wrong by surviving a traumatic event when others did not. We ask, "Why am I alive?" or "What could I have done to prevent this?" For those who live when others suffer and die, there may be guilt about the circumstances of their survival, "It should have been me. I do not deserve to live. I should have been harmed or died with them."

An added dimension of survivor guilt is the paradox of torn emotions. As we encounter our feelings of guilt and shame, secretly we may feel relief and gratitude that we have survived when others did not. Questions about justice, impartiality, and the will of God are part of survivor guilt.

> O LORD, you will hear the desire of the meek;
> you will strengthen their heart, you will incline
> your ear
> to do justice for the orphan and the oppressed,
> so that those from earth may strike terror no more.

—Psalm 10:17-18

Because survivor guilt is of our own creation, it is resolved through the grace of self-forgiveness. Just as the forgiveness of God has no short- or long-term memory, no narrative of guilt, blame, or self-justification is required before we can forgive ourselves. As survivors, forgiveness asks only that we stand in the presence of God and receive the unconditional grace of release from every human emotion that threatens to separate us from the love of God, "So we have known and believe the love that God has for us. God is love, and those who abide in love abide in God, and God abides in them" (1 John 4:16).

PART II

GOD PRESENT WITHIN US

OTHER LOVE

I n grief we are very suggestible. When we grieve, sometimes
we take our emotional cues from the relationship of others
to the one who has died. If *should* takes on larger than life
or larger than death proportions, we set ourselves up for an
experience of grief that feels neither personal nor authentic.

When this happens, we may be conflicted about reality
versus perception. The emotions deeply embedded in our
heart from years of relationship may not always agree with
what others assume has been our experience of the one who
died. If our feelings are at odds or feel somehow misaligned,
it is tempting simply to sink into the bean bag chair of
the status quo and try to find some relatively comfortable
position that will accommodate our emotional load. But
when grief compels us to identify and own what we are
really feeling, we must take a sturdier seat, sit up, and pay
attention to ourselves.

The intuitive reflex of our heart is to love openly, without
reservation. This is how we were born, how we were pre-
programmed for life. If our inward being and outward self
do not match, we may question the very nature of love,
especially when we grieve. Are we able to love? Are we
somehow deficient in love? Are we truly loving in our heart?

When the spontaneous expression of our love is consis-
tently rejected, we question whether what we offer really is

love. Even if there is no fire in our heart, the answer to this question is affirmatively yes. For this is *other* love, which in the end may be the highest and most self-giving love of all. Other love is as important and vital as deep passion, especially when a relationship seems irreparably damaged or defective. Other love allows us to coexist emotionally with the heart of another without chronic conflict and despair.

Other love requires us to be strong and selfless. It is a surprising, self-emptying kind of love that intimates the magnitude of God's love and presence within us. Other love requires us to rise above our personal pain to express the kind of love that transcends conditional limitations. Other love is the stuff of steadfast endurance and irrepressible faith.

Seldom do we give ourselves sufficient credit for finding this kind of other love within our heart. Other love is born of deep, grace-filled compassion, even if we do not feel "real warm affection" (Romans 12:10 PHILLIPS). Compassion is the impulse of our heart to feel the pain and suffering of another, "With everlasting love I will have compassion on you, says the LORD, your Redeemer" (Isaiah 54:8).

Other love is unconditional, freely given from the depths of the human heart, whether it is desired or received. Other love mirrors our inmost character and spiritual integrity.

> Vindicate me, O LORD,
> for I have walked in my integrity,
> and I have trusted in the LORD without wavering.
>
> —Psalm 26:1

Other love inspires us to discover the best of our self, "And this is my prayer, that your love may overflow more and more with knowledge and full insight to help you to determine what is best" (Philippians 1:9-10). Other love refines our soul.

Other love is a sacred response to the presence of God in our lives. Other love costs us nothing.

> The LORD your God is in your midst,
> a mighty one who will save;
> he will rejoice over you with gladness;
> he will quiet you by his love,
> he will exult over you with loud singing.

—Zephaniah 3:17 ESV

SCRAPPY GRIEF

Scrappy grief is the grief of a love that has been turned inside out. Scrappy grief feeds on the fragmented, disconnected, emotional odds and ends of incomplete relationships and unfinished love. When our affections have been misused or extinguished by duty, responsibility, overbearing demands, or disappointed expectations, often we experience this complex variation of grief.

Sometimes we are forced to untangle the brambles of a thorny relationship or clean up the flotsam and jetsam left in the wake of a complicated or broken life. Or we are surprised and heartbroken when we are ambushed by something hidden that changes our perspective or our perception of the one now lost to us in death. If we fail to confront difficult issues of the mind and heart, grief can leave us emotionally handicapped for life.

Scrappy grief makes us take an honest look at what is left of a relationship, or what never was. For some, the absence of real relationship is what we really grieve. Resolving this kind of grief, even in part, requires a certain gritty fortitude which demands that we first confront ourselves, sometimes with the help of an objective third party.

What makes this kind of grief so tenacious and unyielding? Scrappy grief comes from disillusioned love or an ideal of love that may feel more like the opposite of love. Most often, it is rooted within the mixed emotions somewhere in between. Scrappy grief may seem especially daunting because it is about leftover matters of the head and heart that will never be completely resolved.

– We grieve a relationship that might have been, should have been, ought to have been, but never was, and now can never be, "We look before and after... and pine for what is not."[6]

– We grieve the abuse of our love—misspent, squandered, or simply rejected by the one who has died.

– We grieve the emotional connection that should have been, "if only . . ."

– We grieve the death of our hopes and dreams, shattered by the circumstances of life.

Even in healthy relationships, it is hard work to sort through the emotions that inundate us after the death of one we love. It is significantly more difficult to make sense of conflicted emotions, especially if we are wounded by rejection, failed love, or disappointment. We work through the layered emotions of scrappy grief by considering proactive options that align our soul with the presence of God.

– We abandon the past—we disown it; we disclaim it. When we refocus our mind and heart on other, more urgent aspects of our grief, we effectively disempower the past. If we do not nurture the past with our time and energy, it loses its strength and its hold on our life. Over time, the indignities and injustice of the past begin to fade from sheer emotional neglect. A feature of smartphones is an audible whoosh when we send a message to the trash. The message is literally sucked into cyber-oblivion with a noisy reminder that it is now gone—it is history, part of a nanosecond past. Perhaps this small suggestion from technology might inspire us to send some of the past to a mental trash bin, ideally one equipped with an industrial shredder.

– We let go of the past when we live into the present. Perhaps some recent or current event gives us a different perspective on what is really important in life—the birth of a child, remarriage, a health issue, another death, a community tragedy, or even a pandemic or natural disaster. Issues of the past somehow do not seem quite as important when we are fully present to life going on all around us right here, right now.

– We defeat the past when we forgive. It may be difficult, yet in forgiveness there is love. At its most fundamental, grief is an expression of love. Ultimately, it is love that brings us back to personal wholeness. Forgiveness has the power to transcend the damage done to our lives by the one we grieve.

When we experience scrappy grief, sometimes forgiveness is more about relief than resolution. We feel better physically, emotionally, and spiritually when forgiveness is a conscious act of deep, soul-satisfying release. We bless the spirit of another with the gift of human grace when we forgive. Human grace perfectly reflects the power of the presence of God to transform the human heart. The continuous outpouring of God's grace in our lives is the divine gift of love that is unearned, unmerited, and undeserved.

We liberate ourselves from the past when we practice holy forgetfulness, "Love is patient and kind. Love is not jealous or boastful or proud or rude. It does not demand its own way. It is not irritable, and it keeps no record of being wronged" (1 Corinthians 13:4-5 NLT). Forgetting to remember is a discipline—sometimes we must remember to forget. When we do, the weight of our pain, both past and present, begins to lift. It feels lighter, somehow less oppressive. If we are no longer suffocated by the past, we are able at last to grieve forward. Though it does not happen overnight, one day the pain of the past is consigned to a remote corner of our heart, gratefully forgotten through sheer neglect.

When we conquer scrappy grief, we stand triumphantly in the presence of God and claim a hard-won victory over the woundedness in our relationship with the one now lost to us in death, "Let us then lay aside the works of darkness and put on the armor of light" (Romans 13:12).

ON BEING LOVING

A few days after my husband died, I began the slow task of looking through the books he brought home from his office not long after being diagnosed with a terminal illness. Though at the time I did not know exactly what I might find, in my heart I think I was expecting some message or sign that his spirit was still alive and speaking to me.

Although Leighton was a minister, he rarely made notes in his Bibles. As I leafed through his copy of *The New Testament in Modern English* by J. B. Phillips, I found a single verse he had marked, "And above everything else, be truly loving, for love is the golden chain of all the virtues" (Colossians 3:14 PHILLIPS). With the fine point of his Cross pencil he had circled the phrase "truly loving" three times and put an asterisk in the margin beside it. He lived the truth of this verse—he was truly loving.

If the one now lost to us in death was not an object of our great affection, we may devise a kind of personal scorecard to determine whether or not we have measured up in a relationship. If we cannot check the boxes of adoration, warm devotion, and deep love, we pause to consider whether we have succeeded at being loving. If our heart is sincere and we act with love and do that which is loving, we are indeed loving. Though it is not always easy for our spirit to find this place of nobler love, being loving is one of the most honorable things we can do because it is an expression of God's love.

In Scripture, there is an authoritative checklist for the traits and characteristics of being loving, "Love is patient, love is kind. It does not envy, it does not boast, it is not proud. It does not dishonor others, it is not self-seeking, it is not easily angered, it keeps no record of wrongs. Love does not delight in evil but rejoices with the truth. It always protects, always trusts, always hopes, always perseveres. Love never fails" (1 Corinthians 13:4-8 NIV).

- Being loving is resisting the impulse to engage in combative words or arguments. Submission is never surrender.

- Being loving is not noisy. Silence elevates our self-sacrifice and self-giving.

- Being loving is a way of life. We do rather than speak, especially when love is complicated and confusing.

- Being loving sometimes requires extraordinary patience. We wait without expectation of acknowledgment or appreciation.

- Being loving is constructive. It makes something good, positive, or useful out of the remains of a difficult relationship.

- Being loving is not about ownership. Though we may feel suffocated by the overwhelming neediness of the one toward whom we are being loving, we are and will always be our own true selves.

– Being loving is about humility. It is dying to our own self-interest, at least for a while.

– Being loving is about good manners. We are kind, polite, and respectful, even if our urge might be to act and speak in a way that is less than our best self.

– Being loving requires that we concede our hypersensitivity to the moment. We give of ourselves from the grace of who we are.

– Being loving is not about keeping a record of the perceived failures and wrongs of another or of ourselves.

– Being loving is looking for and finding the good—some good, any good—without reservation or judgment.

– Being loving is about endurance, trust, and hope.

Whether we give ourselves high marks or barely passing marks for being loving, this is the love that allows us to release over time every trace of residual resentment, accrued ill-will, and every large or small injustice, whether real or imagined. Though there may never be a final resolution to what we feel about the one we grieve, if we release our spirit from all that has the potential to diminish our heart and tarnish our soul, we experience the blessing of being "truly loving" through the power and presence of God.

> If I speak with the eloquence of men and of angels,
> but have no love, I become no more than blaring
> brass or crashing cymbal. If I have the gift of
> foretelling the future and hold in my mind not

only all human knowledge but the very secrets of
God, and if I also have that absolute faith which
can move mountains, but have no love, I amount to
nothing at all. If I dispose of all that I possess, yes,
even if I give my own body to be burned, but have
no love, I achieve precisely nothing.
This love of which I speak is slow to lose patience—
it looks for a way of being constructive. It is not
possessive: it is neither anxious to impress nor does
it cherish inflated ideas of its own importance.
Love has good manners and does not pursue selfish
advantage. It is not touchy. It does not keep account
of evil or gloat over the wickedness of other people.
On the contrary, it is glad with all good men when
truth prevails.
Love knows no limit to its endurance, no end to its
trust, no fading of its hope; it can outlast anything.
It is, in fact, the one thing that still stands when all
else has fallen . . .
In this life we have three great lasting qualities—
faith, hope and love. But the greatest of them is
love.

—1 Corinthians 13:1-8, 13 PHILLIPS

TROUBLED GRIEF

There is a kind of grief that can only be described as *troubled* if we feel as though an impenetrable semi-gloom has permanently settled over our lives. Troubled grief may seem unshakeable because it is deeply enmeshed in the tangle of our regret, guilt, and unresolved emotions.

Troubled grief is a malaise of mind and spirit that has the power to dictate our every mood and daily disposition toward life. For a while, we may live in complete emotional disarray as we contend with an anguished sense of disorientation to our inmost self. We cannot articulate or explain to others the murky sense of trouble within our soul.

For many, troubled grief feels like an unremitting emotional hangover, a kind of persistent dense brain fog that threatens to impair our functionality on many levels. Somewhere in the depth of our being we intuit that it is not solely the irrefutable fact of death that has left us feeling so troubled, but rather that something in our circumstance feels hopelessly beyond our understanding. Something inside feels irreparably broken.

Troubled grief may be an aftereffect of death if there has been verbal, emotional, or physical abuse in a relationship. After years of emotional ill treatment, a victim may be conditioned to expect the worst in life. For those who were physically or emotionally abandoned at some time in their life by the one who has died, there may be an inescapable feeling that they "did something wrong" and can never make it right, even in death. What if we do not truly mourn the death of the one who has died? How do we reconcile what we think we *ought* to feel with the scars and resentment of our relationship? A cold, tearless grief may arise from a heart taught by experience the dance of mind games, emotional vigilance, mistrust, and self-protection.

How then do we sort out our emotions and resolve the intricacies of troubled grief? Over time, we do the painstaking work of *forensic* grief. That is, we delve into the details of what happened in our life that disturbs and troubles our grief. We identify and name the source of our pain, separate it from other aspects of our life, and begin to connect the cause and effect of our disorientation in grief.

First, we acknowledge that our grief may be troubled beyond our own ability to help ourselves. We may need to seek the help of a medical professional if we live with chronic depression, irritable sadness, or a pervasive sense of general indifference to life. When our grief is troubled, in moments of desperation or dire hopelessness we may whisper to ourself, "I do not care whether I live or die." Or we may ask ourself, "Who is depending on me?" "Who would miss me if I were no longer on this earth?" Quickly, our more rational self intervenes; we cancel these thoughts because they do not honor the God-given life that is ours. A fundamental desire to live and our impulse for self-preservation save us from drastic, unalterable consequences. We take our first step away from troubled grief when we cherish life, "Now choose life, so that you and your children may live and that you may love the LORD your God, listen to his voice, and hold fast to him. For the LORD is your life" (Deuteronomy 30:19b-20b NIV).

Second, we work to sort ourselves out, if necessary, with the guidance of a therapist, trusted clergy, or counselor. When our grief is troubled, it is easy to think ourselves into a pretzel. When we sort ourselves out, we work to untie the knots and straighten out the twists and turns that led us to where we are in our troubled grief. We talk honestly with someone who understands and can give us perspective. We make the conscious decision to live beyond that which cannot be changed or undone. We seek the silence that allows us to listen and hear the voice within our soul. We pray that our spirit will be released from the past. We pray for the peace of God's presence.

Third, we acknowledge that the outcome of our slow, tedious work to resolve our troubled grief will have a positive effect on the rest of our life. We act in real or imagined ways to move forward beyond our experience of grief. We roll the hurt and pain of the past into a tight ball and toss it symbolically into a nearby lake or ocean where it disappears into the depths of the ecosystem. Perhaps we take the same ball and hit it into the stratosphere, where every past pain soars into the universe with hope for the future. Or we make a stronger, more beautiful fabric of our life from the threads of our own self-discovery. Not unlike knitting a sweater, crocheting an afghan, making a needlepoint pillow, or embroidering a dress for a beloved child or grandchild, our work proceeds slowly—stitch by stitch—until we complete the last row, tie the final knot, and discover a design for life that is free from the past. When our work is done, we claim these spiritual truths:

– God never fails us or forsakes us through the
   worst of life's trials. "Be strong and of good
   courage, do not fear or be in dread . . . for it is

the LORD your God who goes with you; he will not fail you or forsake you" (Deuteronomy 31:6 RSV).

– God is trustworthy. "The LORD is a stronghold for the oppressed, a stronghold in times of trouble. And those who know your name put their trust in you, for you, O LORD, have not forsaken those who seek you" (Psalm 9:9-10).

– God gives us strength to withstand and ultimately prevail over life's most daunting relationships and circumstances. "For I, the LORD your God, hold your right hand; it is I who say to you 'Do not fear, I will help you'" (Isaiah 41:13).

– God is gracious. "Turn to me and be gracious to me, for I am lonely and afflicted. Relieve the troubles of my heart, and bring me out of my distress" (Psalm 25:16-17).

– God speaks comfort and peace to our heart. "Let not your heart be troubled" (John 14:1).

Beyond our troubled grief, our strength for today and hope for tomorrow is found only in the presence of God.

You who have done great things O God,
who is like you?
You who have made me see many troubles and calamities
will revive me again;
from the depths of the earth
you will bring me up again.
You will increase my honor,
and comfort me once again.

—Psalm 71:19-21

GRIEF DELAYED

When tragedy and disaster cause the death of a loved one or destroy our home and property, circumstance usually allows little time to do the emotional and spiritual work of grief. We are in crisis mode: those who die are victims, those who survive are victims. Most are emotionally and physically overwhelmed by the basic tasks necessary to make it through even one more day of upheaval and chaos. Yet despite our immeasurable loss, we get up, put one foot in front of the other, and do all we can to sustain life, even as we try to create some order or reason out of what has happened.

When someone we love dies, inevitably we feel the weight of loss that is grief. Yet our first impulse may be to ignore it because our own survival must take precedence, at least for a while. Grief is an inescapable part of loss, whether by death, destruction, divorce, or any other life event that causes the pain of permanent separation. At some time, in some way, we must experience our grief.

How do we recognize grief? At first it may be the persistent ache of dull, relentless sorrow. Grief may feel like a shadow we simply cannot shake or a dark cloud that hovers above us all the time. We cannot eat it away, drink it away, or medicate it away. Grief is there, lurking in the emotional and spiritual background of our lives to remind us that we have not yet come face to face with the depth and breadth of our loss.

Grief can be delayed, but it will not be denied. If you are asking yourself with any regularity, "What is wrong with me?" or "Why do I feel so sad, lonely, angry, or fearful?" likely you are close to an honest encounter with your grief. Once we surrender to our need to grieve, there are no more detours, there is no turning back, "Behold, now is the acceptable time" (2 Corinthians 6:2 ASV).

One of the most faithful members of a grief group was a young man about thirty years old whose beautiful wife had died four years earlier of leukemia. Intuitively, he knew that he had not done the work of grief at the time of her death. For what seemed like the right reasons, he managed to avoid his grief for a while, but at last he was forced to give in to grief's insistent hold on his life. Somewhere along the way, he realized that he could not love another woman again with his whole heart until he had dealt constructively with his grief for his deceased wife. For several months, he shared his heart and persistent sorrow with the group. Over time, he actively engaged with his grief so that at last he felt that he could move forward again with his life.

Sometimes, we must delay our grief, especially when the non-negotiable demands on our life prevent us from responding to our grief—the urgency of our job, the demands of our children or grandchildren, the needs of aging parents, the necessity of rebuilding the physical infrastructure of our life while grappling with questions such as where to live or how to provide for our family when all seems lost.

If we are expected to function and cope despite our grief, we may be forced to hardwire around our feelings for a while so that we are at least physically present to the needs of others and to our own daily life. The outcome of our selflessness may be that we put our grief on hold for months or even years, well beyond the moment of our most immediate pain and sorrow. Grief is patient. It waits for our undivided attention. We may postpone our grief or defer it to some other time, but ultimately we must surrender to its soul-searching power before we are able to live again in true fullness of joy.

At whatever moment we capitulate and fully enter into our grief, the presence of God is continuously at work, moving us forward along the path of life that leads to the restoration of our spirit and rest for our soul.

> Thus says the LORD:
> Stand at the crossroads, and look,
> and ask for the ancient paths,
> where the good way lies; and walk in it,
> and find rest for your souls.
>
> —Jeremiah 6:16

CONVENTION

Most who grieve receive calls, emails, condolence notes, and kind expressions of comfort when a loved one dies. Friends and family respond to our grief in a variety of different ways—some heartfelt, some more perfunctory. The conventions of death and grief and how we reach out to others merit thoughtful consideration, whether we offer or receive comfort.

The herd mentality of twenty-first-century society gladly conforms to convention, especially when someone dies. We send flowers or leave an arrangement at the house of the bereaved. We prepare a meal or bake a cake so the family will not need to be concerned about food or meals. We rummage through our closet to find our black clothes. We dutifully attend the funeral or memorial service and murmur a few awkward words of condolence before we leave. There is almost a cultural formulary for what we do, how we act, and what we say when someone dies.

Yet sometimes we dare the unconventional. Perhaps we choose a private funeral or graveside service if we prefer not to memorialize or celebrate publicly the life of the one we grieve. Or we release butterflies or balloons at an interment or graveside service. Or we scatter the ashes of our loved one somewhere private and meaningful—on a mountaintop, in a garden, or on the water.

If we rethink convention and do something different, those who merely observe rather than participate in our grief are sometimes quick to judge our actions. When a different way of memorializing a loved one runs counter to the more traditional arrangements urged on us by funeral providers or the religious formalities suggested by those who preside over rites and rituals, we may experience some unexpected pushback.

For some, there is solace in strict liturgy, yet we are not bound to do or say the same thing the same way in every situation. When we grieve, sometimes we find new words and ways that go beyond convention and are more appropriate for our particular experience of grief. Many families are personally comforted when a close relative speaks words of remembrance, or a child or grandchild sings a favorite music selection as part of the observance. In these unforgettably comforting moments, a personal bond of love and relationship is honored and shared with the wider community of those who remember and grieve.

Some experience little comfort in traditional, time-worn words of ritual. We free ourselves from the bonds of convention if we take time to craft our inmost thoughts and feelings into a reverent expression of remembrance that is both comfortable and comforting to us. Our prayers and praise to God may flow more freely through personal, heartfelt words that honor the life of one we love with respect, dignity, and the propriety appropriate to our unique experience of grief.

In truth, we are neither duty-bound nor honor-bound to conform to convention. There is no rule book for memorializing a loved one. Even if we expose ourselves to momentary criticism for how we choose to express our grief and direct our own comfort, as long as what we say or do— or do not say or do—is tasteful and appropriate, the surprise and discomfort of others will soon pass and be forgotten. Usually those who judge or criticize participate in our grief for only a short while.

If we are the one in charge of arrangements, we are responsible, first and foremost, for the collective comfort of those who grieve. Though we may choose to do so, we need not depend solely on tried-and-true funeral formats, third-party ideas, or even the advice of clergy professionals. Sometimes we must think for a moment beyond the suggestions of convention to discern what will best care for the emotional well-being of our family and speak to the heart and soul of those who gather together to grieve the death of one they love and remember. God is present to us at this time of spiritual leadership and planning as we seek to provide an experience of authentic comfort for those who grieve, "The human mind plans the way, but the LORD directs the steps" (Proverbs 16:9).

If the life of the one we grieve was noisy or destructive, we may find our comfort in the peace of silence. Or if the one we grieve was a proud veteran who served our country with honor, it may bless our spirit in a special way to hear taps played at the end of a memorial or burial service with military honors. Perhaps we are transported to a place of spiritual oneness with our loved one if a choir sings the "Hallelujah Chorus" from *Messiah* in joyful celebration of a life well lived, "This is my comfort in my distress, that your promise gives me life" (Psalm 119:50).

When we hold fast to the courage of our convictions and dare to challenge the conventions of comfort, we open ourselves to experience new dimensions of the presence of God.

Do not let loyalty and faithfulness forsake you;
bind them around your neck,
write them on the tablet of your heart.

—Proverbs 3:3

FATIGUE

One of the most universal symptoms of grief is fatigue. The almost surreal exhaustion of mind, body, and spirit that overwhelms us when one we love dies may stay with us longer than we might think possible.

Whether we have done battle over time with a debilitating disease, sometimes against insurmountable odds, or we have been present to the slow daily decline of one we love, if we have done the same repetitive job day in and day out to meet the needs of another, over time we realize that we are physically spent. A consequence of caregiving for weeks or months or even years on end is that we access our personal capital to find the strength and stamina required to invest ourselves in the ministry of care, "I know your works, your toil and your patient endurance . . . I also know that you are enduring patiently and bearing up for the sake of my name, and that you have not grown weary" (Revelation 2:2-3).

When one we love dies, it is sometimes a challenge to regain our sense of personal equilibrium because we feel out of balance—physically, mentally, emotionally, and spiritually. Though it may take a while, eventually we recover, regroup, and right ourselves as we return to the rhythm and order of daily life.

As I sat in church a few weeks after my mother died, I realized it was the first time I could remember in what seemed like forever, that I did not feel like there was a large load of worry and anxiety strapped to my heart. Though intellectually I had some perspective on the experience of her death, emotionally I still felt very connected to what was for so long the daily reality of caregiving in my life. It was strangely disorienting no longer to be living in emergency readiness mode every hour of every day.

Expending the necessary physical energy to meet the needs of another person every day at times feels like being on the non-stop treadmill of going and doing. When life ends and the race against circumstance is over, the aftereffect may be a sense of bone-numbing weariness and overwhelming fatigue. When we admit the limitations of our physical and emotional resources, we give ourselves time and space to recover, even if it means letting go of some of the low-priority matters in our life for a while.

How do we recuperate from the fatigue of caregiving as we enter into our grief? By doing the simple things necessary to improve a little each day. We get up. We get dressed. We have at least one well-balanced, nourishing meal. We move our body. We have a real conversation with at least one other person and reconnect with the world. We laugh. We learn how to relax again. We rest. We nap. We sleep.

Rather than attempting too much all at once, we settle down and settle in. For a while, we may have no burning interests because we have given so much to others. We have difficulty concentrating on reading or other resources that may add to our comfort. And so, we speak less and think more. We reflect on both the stress and the satisfaction of self-giving. We listen for the voice of God within the quiet of our soul. We renew our strength in the certainty that God is present to us as we grieve.

Even youths will faint and be weary,
and the young shall fall exhausted;
but those who wait for the LORD shall renew their
strength,
they shall mount up with wings like eagles,
they shall run and not be weary,
they shall walk and not faint.

—Isaiah 40:30-31

Come to me, all of you who are weary and over-
burdened, and I will give you rest! Put on my yoke
and learn from me. For I am gentle and humble in
heart and you will find rest for your souls. For my
yoke is easy and my burden is light.

—Matthew 11:28-30 PHILLIPS

INTERMITTENT GRIEF

When we grieve, though we may be physically present in situations that require us to engage with others, it is quite normal to feel emotionally absent. At the first meeting I attended after the death of my mother, I remember thinking how good it felt to be part of something larger than myself again. As I participated in the business of the day, I saw others and listened to their words. The man sitting next to me sputtered some well-intended words of condolence punctuated by a small, uncomfortable laugh. In what seemed like an out-of-body experience, I realized that no one could possibly imagine the emptiness of my subdued spirit. My sense of detachment from the group that day made me acutely aware of being on the loss side of the veil that separates life from death.

After the meeting, I felt strangely disturbed and realized that being in a medical setting had roiled my subconscious. Without warning, a corner of my mind had flashed back to the illness and death that were still very fresh in my heart. I was more than a little surprised that this painful reminder had such a sharp effect on my still-fragile spirit.

Intermittent grief is the faithful tap-tap-tapping on the window of our soul that gets our attention and transports us to the place of personal grief forever reserved for the one we love. Long after the tears of shock subside and we begin to think that we are better, time and again grief reaches into our heart to remind us of our loss. It surprises us, especially when we are unprepared to deal with it.

I was overwhelmed one evening by a television program in which a mother and daughter were reunited after a two-year separation. Their wordless embrace perfectly expressed the unbroken bond of their love. In the power of that moment, my eyes filled with tears because I longed to have had that kind of relationship with my own mother. Though I grieved what was *not* while my mother was alive, the sheer tenacity of intermittent grief always takes my breath away.

Intermittent grief may be triggered by our heightened sense of associative recall. The smallest token, a slight gesture, or a shared place unexpectedly reminds us of the one now lost to us in death. Though we may think we have done the heart and mind work of grief, if we are suddenly confronted by something large or small that cues our emotions, the memory of our heart skips directly to the feelings we associate with a particular experience or moment in time. When this happens, we are forced by grief to pause, reflect, and honor the sadness or sorrow or joy of a sacred experience that resides forever in our heart.

On a beautiful Sunday morning, the church choir sang "One Faith, One Hope, One Lord." My husband loved this anthem; it was sung when he retired from a long-term pastorate and later at his memorial service. With the first notes of the organ, my heart dissolved as I thought of him and remembered the powerful occasions in our life associated with that music. In a twinkling moment, I sensed him there beside me, loving me, comforting me. A memory of the unforgettable was transformed into a joyful reunion of our souls.

If we enter into moments of intermittent grief without explanation or apology for our emotional reaction or tears, we have an authentic encounter with the depth of our soul. We are comforted every time we remember the love we have known and will forever share with the one now lost to us in death, "You have granted me life and steadfast love, and your care has preserved my spirit" (Job 10:12). We grieve because we love—love that delights us, love that surprises us, love that pains us, love that disappoints us. As we discover our heart's own rhythm of growth and restoration to life, intermittent grief is a faithful reminder that love never dies.

We experience intermittent grief because it is not humanly possible to resolve the heartfelt emotions of life and death and grief once and for all time. As with intermittent grief, we return again and again to experience comfort and life-renewing strength in the presence of God.

Yet even now, says the Lord,
return to me with all your heart,
with fasting, with weeping, and with mourning;

Return to the LORD, your God,
for he is gracious and merciful.

—Joel 2:12-13

MY LIFE IS A WRECK

From time to time, I receive emails from strangers who reach out from their place of anonymity in search of a listening ear or a word of encouragement to survive a moment of despair in their grief. Usually their plea for help comes at a late hour from the abyss of pain and sorrow that is the dark night of the soul, "How long must I bear pain in my soul, and have sorrow in my heart all day long?" (Psalm 13:2). Often those who write are mothers whose children have died unexpectedly from tragic, preventable causes.

One mother's son died from inhalant abuse. Another mother's son died of a drug overdose. Another mother shared the tragic circumstances of her daughter's death from cancer and the death of her two nieces, all within a short period of time. Recently, one woman poured out the agonized story of her beloved son's death from an opioid overdose. Her message ended with the anguished cry, "My life is a wreck." As with most mothers, her son was the bright and shining star of her life. She was completely bereft because she felt that the senseless, untimely death of her beloved son had wrecked her life.

When one we love dies, suddenly our dreams, our hopes, and our aspirations come crashing down around us. Whether our life has been wrecked over a period of weeks or months by a deteriorating situation, or abruptly by an unexpected, tragic accident or event, the result is usually the same—a part of our heart feels irreparably destroyed by the death of one we love. At least for a while, our life may feel like a wreck.

Consider the parallel of a violent, destructive train wreck. For some unforeseen reason, within mere seconds cars of every variety jump the track and pile up at odd angles. In an instant, what was once a means of transportation becomes a twisted mass of wreckage. The train is still a train, but in the aftermath of disaster, it is little more than a crumpled heap of metal that only faintly suggests its former intended function.

Or envision a heavy metal wrecking ball swinging from a crane. With one or more precisely targeted blows it accomplishes its sole purpose: the total demolition of a building. Remarkably, the whole still exists after the job is complete, but only as a large pile of construction rubble. While the millions of small pieces can never be reassembled into the structure that was destroyed, that which is salvageable can be repurposed into the gravel, concrete, cement, or mortar that will one day be used as the building blocks of a new structure. Energy and new life can come from destruction. The same crane that swings the wrecking ball also lifts the wreckage of a train crash—that which destroys can also rescue and build up.

Grief is sometimes driven by a sense of urgency to understand what happened to wreck our lives. Perhaps we delve into the cause of death and learn all we can about a disease, an addiction, or the behavior that may have been the cause of death. We struggle until we are able to reconcile ourselves to the fact that there will always be unanswered questions. To live and move forward, we must consign the unknowable to that corner of our heart reserved by grief for acceptance.

How do we find life beyond the emotional wreckage of death? We resolve to make a difference in the world so that perhaps just one other person will not have to experience the same pain and suffering that we and others who survive have endured and overcome. In faith, we do the work required to clear the wreckage from our life and rebuild a life refined by tragedy into a life enlarged by our experience of death and grief.

– We resist the urge to assign blame to someone or something.

– We forgive ourselves whatever guilt may taunt or convict us. "I will never forgive myself" keeps us buried in the wreckage. In forgiveness, we experience the presence of God.

– We believe that love and relationships never die, "Love knows no limit to its endurance, no end to its trust, no fading of its hope; it can outlast anything. It is, in fact, the one thing that still stands when all else has fallen" (1 Corinthians 13:7-8 PHILLIPS).

– We discover the vast reserve of courage, strength, and resilience within our own spiritual character, "Seek the LORD and his strength, seek his presence continually. Remember the wonderful works he has done" (1 Chronicles 16:11-12).

– We give thanks for the presence of God that empowers us to rebuild our life from the wreckage of grief, "The LORD has heard my supplication; the LORD accepts my prayer" (Psalm 6:9).

For everything there is a season, and a time for
every matter under heaven:
a time to be born, and a time to die;
a time to plant, and a time to pluck up what is
planted;
a time to kill, and a time to heal;
a time to break down, and a time to build up;
a time to weep, and a time to laugh;
a time to mourn, and a time to dance;
a time to throw away stones, and a time to gather
stones together;
a time to embrace, and a time to refrain from
embracing;
a time to seek, and a time to lose;
a time to keep, and a time to throw away;
a time to tear, and a time to sew;
a time to keep silence, and a time to speak;
a time to love, and a time to hate;
a time for war, and a time for peace.

—Ecclesiastes 3:1-8

DISAPPOINTED HOPE

There is a vast chasm between the ordinary small and large disappointments of daily life and the total rupture of disappointed hope. The disappointments of those on the near side of the chasm most often have one thing in common—people. Generally, we react within a limited bandwidth of emotions to normal, predictable disappointments that occur in the rhythm of everyday life. Though our initial response to disappointment may be anger or sadness, above all else disappointment is painful. It hurts because it is personal.

We are bitterly disappointed if the vows of our marriage are betrayed. We are disappointed when the bright vision we cherish for our children is dimmed by wrong choices that lead to tragedy or alienation. We are disappointed with ourselves when we lose a job or our application to a preferred school is not accepted. In these moments of seeming failure, self-reproach fuels our disappointment. Disappointment easily blocks other avenues that promise greater potential for the future.

On the far side of the chasm of disappointed hope is the life-altering experience of death. Is there anything that has the power to affect our human heart and spirit more than the death of one we love? No, surely not. No disappointment or treachery in life inherently possesses the same brute force or crushing power to wound us as does death. When one we love dies, disappointment can take on a life of its own.

The parable of the prodigal son is a complex story about personal choice and disappointed hope. On both sides of the chasm there is disappointed hope with the added sidebar of injustice, as expressed by the self-righteous indignation of the elder brother. While the more obvious themes of the illustration are selfishness, greed, and envy, the spiritual themes that ultimately teach us the lesson of the parable are love, joy, forgiveness, and redemption.

> There was a man who had two sons. The younger
> of them said to his father, 'Father, give me the
> share of the property that will belong to me.' So he
> divided his property between them. A few days later
> the younger son gathered all he had and traveled
> to a distant country, and there he squandered his
> property in dissolute living. When he had spent
> everything, a severe famine took place throughout
> that country, and he began to be in need. So he
> went and hired himself out to one of the citizens
> of that country, who sent him to his fields to feed
> the pigs. He would gladly have filled himself with
> the pods that the pigs were eating; and no one gave
> him anything. But when he came to himself he
> said, 'How many of my father's hired hands have
> bread enough and to spare, but here I am dying of
> hunger! I will get up and go to my father, and I will
> say to him, "Father, I have sinned against heaven
> and before you; I am no longer worthy to be called
> your son; treat me like one of your hired hands."' So
> he set off and went to his father. But while he was
> still far off, his father saw him and was filled with

compassion; he ran and put his arms around him and kissed him. Then the son said to him, 'Father, I have sinned against heaven and before you; I am no longer worthy to be called your son.' But the father said to his slaves, 'Quickly, bring out a robe—the best one—and put it on him; put a ring on his finger and sandals on his feet. And get the fatted calf and kill it, and let us eat and celebrate; for this son of mine was dead and is alive again; he was lost and is found!' And they began to celebrate.
Now his elder son was in the field; and when he came and approached the house, he heard music and dancing. He called one of the slaves and asked what was going on. He replied, 'Your brother has come, and your father has killed the fatted calf, because he has got him back safe and sound.' Then he became angry and refused to go in. His father came out and began to plead with him. But he answered his father, 'Listen! For all these years I have been working like a slave for you, and I have never disobeyed your command; yet you have never given me even a young goat so that I might celebrate with my friends. But when this son of yours came back, who has devoured your property with prostitutes, you killed the fatted calf for him!' Then the father said to him, 'Son, you are always with me, and all that is mine is yours. But we had to celebrate and rejoice, because this brother of yours was dead and has come to life; he was lost and has been found.'
—Luke 15:11-32

The younger son is described as *prodigal* because he was wasteful and extravagant. He did not want to wait for his inheritance—he wanted to live in the moment and enjoy life now. When he decided to leave the comfort and safety of home, he shattered his father's hopes and dreams for his life. And though the irreverence of the younger son and his disregard for heritage and tradition disappointed the hope of the father, he allowed his son to leave home and experience the inevitable consequences of making bad choices. According to the narrative, the father acknowledged more than once the possibility that his younger son might even be dead.

Yet in an instant, the father's disappointed hope turned to joy when his lost son returned, "for this son of mine was dead and is alive again; he was lost and is found!" The prodigal was restored to his place in the household by a loving father without judgment, commentary, or condemnation of his foray into the world.

On the near side of the chasm of disappointed hope the elder son was disgruntled and angry at his father. He was disappointed not by the return of his brother, but by how his brother was celebrated. As the faithful stay-at-home son, the steady plodder of the family, his life was about obedience and duty. He was understandably disappointed by his father's preferential treatment of the wayward younger son and the seeming inequity of the situation. In this story of disappointed hope, the elder son expected justice. Instead, his father offered love and mercy reconciled by the grace of God.

When we weigh our disappointment over the death of the one we love against the sacred gift of our own life, grief teaches us that it is not a betrayal of our loved one to be joyful. In every circumstance of life, joy bridges the chasm of disappointed hope because joy comes from within. The presence of God continually urges us to live in fullness of joy beyond our disappointed hope, "Weeping may linger for the night, but joy comes with the morning" (Psalm 30:5).

A HEART OF STONE

I will give them one heart, and put a new spirit
within them; I will remove the heart of stone from
their flesh and give them a heart of flesh.
—Ezekiel 11:19

When one we love dies, it is not unusual to feel the weight
of a kind of chest pain that defies description. The
logical assumption is that our pain could be symptomatic of
a serious medical condition. When we grieve, it is especially
important to consult a physician if any kind of unfamiliar
discomfort gets our attention. Though what we are feeling
may be simply a physical manifestation of the emotional
pain of grief, there is a very real connection between our
heart, our mind, and our physical body which should never
be underestimated or dismissed when one we love dies.

My husband died after a sudden, unexpected, and
relatively short illness. He did not die from the diagnosed
disease, but rather from a series of medical errors made
by a dispassionate healthcare institution. The traumatic
experience of the death of my beloved husband left me with
a textbook "heart of stone."

Not long after he died, frequent episodes of chest pain
and shortness of breath sounded the alarm that something
might be physically wrong with my heart. On a Friday
afternoon, I found myself in a physician's office hooked up to

stress test monitors and a treadmill. Though the tests showed nothing out of the ordinary, overwhelming grief weighed so heavily on my heart, I thought that surely I must be having a heart attack.

Perhaps shock kept my heart of stone intact for a while. Soon enough, the inevitable force of emotional gravity took its natural course. One day, my heart of stone fell unceremoniously into the depths of grief and broke into a million small pieces.

In truth, the heart of stone is a kind of reflexive, self-protective grief mechanism that for a while may render our human emotions unyielding and self-contained. We feel immobilized by the sheer weightiness of the death of one we love. The heart of stone moment in grief allows us to isolate our feelings so that we may begin to deconstruct the complexities of our grief, "a time to throw away stones, and a time to gather stones together; a time to embrace, and a time to refrain from embracing" (Ecclesiastes 3:5).

Perhaps the immovable stone we feel in our heart is really only a block of ice that slowly melts when its solid form and hard exterior gain heat. As the block of ice begins to thaw and its sharp edges soften, it slowly reduces in size, though the volume remains constant. As the mass liquefies, it gradually returns to its former state—pure water. Not unlike a block of ice, we must thaw and melt in order to rejoin the world. As grief changes its shape and form in our lives and life becomes more fluid, we use the cool, fresh water from our melted heart of stone to rehydrate our spirit and cleanse our soul.

A sculptor has the God-given talent and ability to stand in front of a piece of raw stone and see with the eye of an artist the shape of the figure that will one day emerge from its rough exterior. With each tap of the chisel, a piece of stone takes on life and form. To resolve some of the issues and emotions of grief, we may need to chip away at our heart of stone using the tools of faith.

- We pray for relief from the weight of that which cannot be changed, "The LORD is my rock, my fortress, and my deliverer, my God, my rock in whom I take refuge, my shield, and the horn of my salvation, my stronghold" (Psalm 18:2).

- We hope for a future beyond the rigid apathy of our heart of stone, "Listen to advice and accept instruction, that you may gain wisdom for the future" (Proverbs 19:20).

- We live into the kindness and compassion that returns us to humanity, "Whoever pursues righteousness and kindness will find life and honor" (Proverbs 21:21).

Through the presence of God, our heart of stone is transformed into a heart of flesh that is our own new life, "A new heart I will give you, and a new spirit I will put within you; and I will remove from your body the heart of stone and give you a heart of flesh" (Ezekiel 36:26).

DRESSING
FOR GRIEF

Why is it that when someone we love dies, one of our first thoughts may be about what we will wear to the funeral, graveside ceremony, or memorial service? Intuitively, we know that our outward appearance should correspond to the solemnity of the observance, whether our customs are ancient and formal, or modern and more informal. We rummage through our closet, or perhaps even go shopping to find the *right* thing to wear, something quiet and somber that appropriately honors a sacred remembrance of life and death.

Occasionally, we read an obituary notice, an online condolence page, or a post on social media that asks those who plan to attend a memorial or funeral service to wear a favorite color of the deceased or one that is emblematic of a cause or disease closely associated with the one who has died. And though there are no hard and fast *rules*, dark colors are more traditional in Western culture, while in other parts of the world bright colors are the dress standard for mourning—white in Middle Eastern cultures, blue in Korea, yellow in Egypt and Ethiopia, to name only a few.

Though traditions, social mores, and standards of conformity vary from culture to culture, in our contemporary world, dressing for grief is sometimes intended to mitigate sadness. The unspoken message is, "Celebrate! Don't be sad!" Whether this is a sentiment that was expressed by the deceased or one that reflects the brave determination of those who survive, there is no shortcut around grief, no matter what we are wearing—black from head to toe, a jaunty tie, theme socks, or a brightly colored outfit. The sincere, well-intentioned devices and gimmicks that suggest we should somehow subdue our sorrow and set aside our sadness belie the fundamental need of every human being to grieve.

When death robs us of joy because the person who was once the object of our human love and affection is no longer here, it is a normal response of grief to resist the outward expression of emotions that we are not feeling inwardly. Instinctively, something deep within our broken heart refuses to fake our emotional well-being—it is difficult to pretend that we are happy when we are not. It simply may not be possible to wear a bright sweater at Christmas, or anything festive at any other time that sends a contradictory message about the state of our broken heart.

Though we seldom wear the symbolic sackcloth of mourning common to some traditions, at least for a while, our sad, anonymous clothes may feel safe and comfortable, perhaps even comforting until we decide that we are ready to mirror a more encouraged soul through something as ordinary as our daily dress.

When life as we know it is irrevocably changed by the death of one we love, we are stripped naked of our perceived independence, self-reliance, self-determination, and the skin-tight control with which we routinely navigate life. The frailty and humanness of our soul and spirit are laid bare for all the world to see when we are suddenly undressed emotionally by death.

How, then, do we re-dress our grief? *Redress* means to set right, to remedy, or to relieve. *Redress* also means to adjust something such as balance, to a state of evenness. When one we love dies, the counter-balance principle of equal and opposite relationship is forever altered. As we endeavor to redress our grief, over time we seek to rebalance our life from without and within, "and to clothe yourselves with the new self, created according to the likeness of God in true righteousness and holiness" (Ephesians 4:24).

Redress in grief begins with identifying areas of imbalance in our life. Is our family dynamic suddenly skewed by the death of a husband or father, a wife or mother? Are we worried about our personal care and provision? Are we caught off balance when we are deprived of physical affection and cannot express our human sexuality? One of the challenges of grief is learning how to recalibrate ourselves and our lives. How do we fill the void left by the one we love and relieve our emptiness? How do we restore the emotional and spiritual balance in our life? We look inside the lost-and-found of our soul and do the work necessary to redress our grief through introspection and self-examination. When we suffer from extreme imbalance, we seek the perspective of an experienced advisor who can guide us through the redress of our loss and grief.

The effect of grief on our life is never passive. Either we actively grow from our grief and through our grief, or we shrink into grief, conforming our shell to the unalterable circumstance of death. If grief drives us forward in life, inevitably we become a size larger in our soul—no elastic waistband required. What does the redress of grief look like? What does the redress of grief feel like? What does grief teach us to wear?

- A heart of trust, "But if God so clothes the grass
  of the field, which is alive today and tomorrow
  is thrown into the oven, will he not much more
  clothe you—you of little faith?" (Matthew 6:30).

- A mind enlarged by a deeper understanding of
  grief, "Blessed are those who mourn, for they will
  be comforted" (Matthew 5:4).

- A soul sensitized to the grief of others in the
  world, "He has caused his wonders to be remembered; the LORD is gracious and compassionate"
  (Psalm 111:4 NIV).

- A spirit of confidence in the certainty that life
  triumphs over death, "for whatever is born of God
  conquers the world. And this is the victory that
  conquers the world, our faith" (1 John 5:4).

When we at last put away our well-worn grief wardrobe,
we are redressed in a garment of thanksgiving and praise for
the presence of God.

In the beginning, Lord, you founded the earth,
and the heavens are the work of your hands;
they will perish, but you remain;
they will all wear out like clothing;
like a cloak you will roll them up,
and like clothing they will be changed.
But you are the same,
and your years will never end.
—Hebrews 1:10-12

Therefore take up the whole armor of God, so that
you may be able to withstand on that evil day,

and having done everything, to stand firm. Stand therefore, and fasten the belt of truth around your waist, and put on the breastplate of righteousness. As shoes for your feet put on whatever will make you ready to proclaim the gospel of peace. With all of these, take the shield of faith, with which you will be able to quench all the flaming arrows of the evil one. Take the helmet of salvation, and the sword of the Spirit, which is the word of God.

—Ephesians 6:13-17

ASHES

In a particularly tragic event on March 3, 2017 a fire brutally ripped through a sixty-unit condominium complex in Dallas, Texas. Residents rushed from their homes at midnight with nothing on except the clothes they were wearing, mostly pajamas, robes, and night clothes. Only a few people were able to grab a handbag or cellphone on the way out. Almost one hundred residents, mostly retirees, were suddenly standing on the sidewalk on an unseasonably cold night, dazed and in shock, permanently displaced from the comfort of their homes. It was later discovered that an elderly woman with dementia had died in the blaze.

More than one hundred firefighters worked through the night to douse the flames. For the next two days, they continued their work by stirring through the ashes to ensure that there were no smoldering remains. When at last the smoke cleared, the condo building was assessed as a total loss—nothing was salvageable. The possessions of a lifetime, each with a story of love and life and loss, were reduced to a pile of gray ash amid the charred structural steel that was once home to so many. Not unlike a forest stripped bare by a raging fire, the picture of ruin was naked, ugly, and desolate.

When one we love dies, we may feel as though our entire life is in ruins. Sometimes we say that our life has "gone up in smoke." Everything so lovingly built over a lifetime has been destroyed in an instant by death. Long after the one we love dies, we may continue to sift through the lifeless ashes of loss for some still-live cinder of understanding or a small spark of insight.

Emotional and spiritual ashes are a very real byproduct of grief. Unwittingly, we may churn the ashes of our inmost heart at the risk of reigniting unextinguished embers better left unstirred. We may find the cold pain of an exhausted relationship within the lifeless ashes, or the warm glow of a love that will never die.

Over a long Memorial Day weekend, a series of related, yet oddly disconnected remembrances, thoughts, and subtle reminders cascaded through my mind. On an overcast Sunday afternoon, quite unexpectedly I found myself in a dark emotional place pawing through the ashes of the past—correspondence, photos, fiery emails. I spent the afternoon on the hearth of yesterday and discovered for my trouble nothing more than the cold, powdery residue of the past. I realized yet again that in some relationships, I simply did not succeed in getting life right all the time with all people. By the end of the day, I was a sooty mess—I could do nothing more than dust myself off, say a simple prayer of release and forgiveness, and return to the beauty of life in the here and now.

Historically, ashes have sometimes served as an outward, visible sign of grief. One who was grieving either sat in the ashes of burned wood as a sign of desolation, or ashes were sprinkled over the head and body as a recognizable convention that wordlessly demonstrated grief, "Then I turned to the Lord God, to seek an answer by prayer and supplication with fasting and sackcloth and ashes" (Daniel 9:3).

Many are especially attuned to the personal significance of ashes because a loved one has been cremated. We may experience a certain chill finality when we are handed an urn that contains the ashes of one whose mortal body has been burned, "He has cast me into the mire, and I have become like dust and ashes" (Job 30:19). If we are charged with honoring the wishes of one whose life we cherish and hold dear, we may have the privilege, or perhaps the obligation, to faithfully dispose of ashes in a way that is respectful, meaningful, and personal, "earth to earth, ashes to ashes, dust to dust."[7] This may be an exhilarating experience of sacred communion, a stoic duty of death, or a simple acknowledgment of ashes as a symbol of the earth to which all living things return when they die and from which new life springs.

Ashes, whether symbolic or real, are a part of grief. As we carefully sift through the ashes of our sorrow, the presence of God stirs our soul and rekindles our spirit to new life.

> You have turned my mourning into dancing;
> you have taken off my sackcloth
> and clothed me with joy,
> so that my soul may praise you and not be silent.
> O LORD my God, I will give thanks to you forever.
>
> —Psalm 30:11-12

INCONSOLABLE

One of the most fragile corners of our grief is the private place where we are completely inconsolable. Though this is not where we reside for an extended period of time, it is a place of spiritual disorientation where we do battle with our sense of abandonment and isolation, even as we defend the crumbling fortress of our heart.

> Be gracious to me, O Lord, for I am in distress;
> my eye wastes away from grief,
> my soul and body also.
> For my life is spent with sorrow,
> and my years with sighing;
> my strength fails because of my misery,
> and my bones waste away.
> —Psalm 31:9-10

If we separate ourselves from others either emotionally or physically, we cannot be reached by anyone or anything. When we withdraw from the world, sometimes for our own self-preservation, we tacitly reject every word or gesture offered to comfort us in our brokenness. As we succumb to our woundedness, for a while we are inaccessible, shut down, out of business. A *closed* sign in large letters cannot be missed by those who seek to retrieve or rescue us from this dark place of grief.

When we are inconsolable, our perspective is a little like looking through the wrong end of a telescope—we can focus on nothing other than our indescribable pain to the exclusion of every expression of human care and concern.

> In the day of my trouble I seek the Lord;
> in the night my hand is stretched out without
> wearying;
> my soul refuses to be comforted.
> I think of God and I moan;
> I meditate, and my spirit faints.

—Psalm 77:2-3

This place of emotional self-exile is devoid of the potential for healing offered by solitude. Rather, it is a lonely place that threatens to detach us permanently from all we hold dear in life.

> Thus says the LORD:
> A voice is heard in Ramah,
> lamentation and bitter weeping.
> Rachel is weeping for her children;
> she refuses to be comforted for her children,
> because they are no more.

—Jeremiah 31:15

It is unaccustomed and disconcerting when we feel utterly inconsolable. If we lose our sense of direction in a dark body of water, we are unnerved by a momentary sense of disorientation. If we resist the impulse to panic, we look for direction. At first, we follow our own air bubbles as they rise through the water. Only when we focus on the light that shines through the dark murk of grief do we see the way to rise to the surface and return to life, "for the LORD will be your everlasting light, and your days of mourning shall be ended" (Isaiah 60:20).

As we move away from our self-imposed loneliness, our transition from feeling inconsolable to opening our hearts to trust again in others usually occurs gradually.

Will the Lord spurn forever,
and never again be favorable?
Has his steadfast love ceased forever?
Are his promises at an end for all time?
Has God forgotten to be gracious?
Has he in anger shut up his compassion?" . . .
And I say, "It is my grief
that the right hand of the Most High has changed.

—Psalm 77:7-10

How do we move through an inconsolable time of grief?

– We pray because we know that God answers our prayers. "Hear my prayer, O God; give ear to the words of my mouth" (Psalm 54:2).

– We allow the faithful prayers of others to support us in the reconciling work of grief. "The LORD is near to the brokenhearted, and saves the crushed in spirit" (Psalm 34:18).

– We believe in the power of God to console us, even when we feel inconsolable. "My soul melts away for sorrow; strengthen me according to your word" (Psalm 119:28).

– We learn again to hope.
I will call to mind the deeds of the LORD;
I will remember your wonders of old.
I will meditate on all your work,
and muse on your mighty deeds.
Your way, O God, is holy.
What god is so great as our God?
You are the God who works wonders;
you have displayed your might among the peoples.

—Psalm 77:11-14

The source of our consolation is the presence of God. God is with us, always, "When the cares of my heart are many, your consolations cheer my soul" (Psalm 94:19).

If we are being afflicted, it is for your consolation
and salvation; if we are being consoled, it is for
your consolation, which you experience when you
patiently endure the same sufferings that we are also
suffering. Our hope for you is unshaken; for we
know that as you share in our sufferings, so also you
share in our consolation.

—2 Corinthians 1:6-7

INVISIBLE

At some time, most everyone who grieves experiences moments of feeling invisible, that sense of *otherness* when one we love dies. For example, have you been to a restaurant by yourself and been made to feel as though you were invisible? After a wait that suggests you have been all but forgotten, you are seated at one of the tables near the restroom or kitchen that seem to be permanently reserved for those who eat alone. It is not unusual for those in the hospitality industry to treat solo diners like second-class citizens by offering little more than poor service at a forgotten table.

Or have you been to a party where it seemed easier or perhaps less awkward simply to stand in a corner like a potted plant and try to be invisible? On such occasions, sometimes we dress so that we do not call attention to ourselves. As we stand there, we listen to the looping solo conversation playing in our head, "Why am I here? I do not really want to talk to anyone. When can I leave?" If we are struggling to find a sense of personal equanimity after the death of one we love, social situations can be an ongoing challenge. Though it is not the responsibility of others to sense or understand our needs when we grieve, sometimes we do not have the reserves to be more than our wounded self, and so we retreat to a place of emotional invisibility for a while.

The experience of grief allows us to see ourselves like never before, as the imperfect, fallible human beings that we are—it is impossible to be invisible in the first person. Because complete personal transparency is a gift of grief, if we look within we see through ourselves and discover by introspection and prayer more about who we are spiritually, perhaps for the first time in life, "Answer me when I call, O God of my right! You gave me room when I was in distress. Be gracious to me, and hear my prayer" (Psalm 4:1).

In nature, the life cycle begins with a seed that sprouts and grows into a mature plant. It then produces the flowers that ultimately yield seeds that propagate and begin the cycle again, "Ever since the creation of the world his eternal power and divine nature, invisible though they are, have been understood and seen through the things he has made" (Romans 1:20).

The invisible work of nature that happens below the soil line is nothing short of miraculous, "By faith we understand that the worlds were prepared by the word of God, so that what is seen was made from things that are not visible" (Hebrews 11:3). During the cycle of grief that ends in our return to fulness of life, God works invisibly to grow us so that we may again blossom and bear fruit, "You will know them by their fruits" (Matthew 7:16).

 - Plants need water to grow. We know that it is
   time to water plants when the soil is visibly dry,
   "The waters nourished it, the deep made it grow
   tall, making its rivers flow around the place it was
   planted, sending forth its streams to all the trees
   of the field" (Ezekiel 31:4).

– Plants need nutrients from the soil that are taken up through the roots. When we grieve, we need spiritual nurture for our soul to thrive, "Then God said, 'Let the earth put forth vegetation: plants yielding seed, and fruit trees of every kind on earth that bear fruit with the seed in it'" (Genesis 1:11).

– Plants need fresh, clean air to grow and fertile soil that supports the plant and anchors the roots, "But as for that in the good soil, these are the ones who, when they hear the word, hold it fast in an honest and good heart, and bear fruit with patient endurance" (Luke 8:15).

– Plants need the energy of sunlight. In an environment where the light is weak or insufficient, a plant cannot flourish—it produces fewer flowers and less fruit, "For the LORD God is a sun and shield; he bestows favor and honor. No good thing does the LORD withhold from those who walk uprightly" (Psalm 84:11).

– Plants need room to grow. Without adequate space, the roots and foliage of overcrowded plants are stunted in their growth, "You water its furrows abundantly, settling its ridges, softening it with showers, and blessing its growth" (Psalm 65:10).

– Plants require time; they do not grow overnight. Each plant requires a certain number of days, months, or even years to be productive, "The earth brought forth vegetation: plants yielding seed of every kind, and trees of every kind bearing fruit with the seed in it. And God saw that it was good" (Genesis 1:12).

Our grief is transformed by the presence of God at work in our lives in ways unknown and unseen to us, "I will set my eyes upon them for good . . . I will plant them, and not pluck them up" (Jeremiah 24:6). In the presence of God, we grow where we are planted.

PART III

GOD PRESENT THROUGH US

A NEW HEART

Short of a transplant, most would agree that there is no way to get a new physical heart. Even a transplanted heart is secondhand and usually comes with some wear and tear. The closest any of us ever come to having a new heart is when we are born. Yet even when we come into the world with our first breath of life, our hearts have been in development for a full nine months.

The spiritual heart is the natural wellspring of our thoughts, our will, our emotions, and sometimes even our motivations. It is perhaps the most personal and vulnerable part of the human soul—the heart is at the core of our inmost being. When we grieve, even our heart longs for a new heart. We want our brokenness fixed. We long for a heart that feels whole, fully functional, and restored to life, "Create in me a clean heart, O God, and put a new and right spirit within me" (Psalm 51:10).

The requirements for a physical organ transplant inform our spiritual desire for a new heart:

– A new heart must be clean. A donor heart must have no history of trauma or cardiac disease and test within normal ranges. In other words, we must determine the criteria for our own new heart and purge leftover damage, guilt, and emotional

toxins that are responsible for our momentary
sense of spiritual infirmity, "Truly God is good
to the upright, to those who are pure in heart"
(Psalm 73:1)

— A new heart must be free of congenital defects.
A congenital heart defect is a problem with the
structure of the heart, usually present at birth.
Some may live with certain emotional defects
modeled or taught from birth. We observe and
learn certain behaviors from those entrusted
with the care and nurture of our heart. Some can
have a negative effect on our heart for life. Our
spiritual quest for a new heart must transcend
both our cultural and family conditioning,
"Do not be conformed to this world, but be
transformed by the renewing of your minds,
so that you may discern what is the will of
God—what is good and acceptable and perfect"
(Romans 12:2).

— A new heart must have a normal rhythm. The
job of the physical heart is to pump blood to the
body. When it is functioning properly, the heart
pumps with a regular, steady beat about 100,000
times per day, between sixty and one-hundred
times per minute. A normal heartbeat is produced
by both physical and electrical energy. When we
grieve, we are attuned to a range of emotional ups
and down that can affect both the physical and
spiritual rhythm of our heart. In truth, grief is
perhaps the most arrhythmic experience of body
and soul that will ever challenge the rhythmic
order of our life. A new heart finds its own

rhythm, "get yourselves a new heart and a new spirit!" (Ezekiel 18:31).

"How long can I live with a new heart?" is a common question asked by many heart transplant recipients. For those whose hearts are broken by the death of one they love, the simple answer is, forever. For at the heart of God we find our own new heart. Through the presence of God, our old, grief-worn heart is transformed into a new heart, a grateful heart that pulses with spiritual vitality and praise, "I give thanks to you, O Lord my God, with my whole heart, and I will glorify your name forever" (Psalm 86:12).

REFLEXIVE GOD

No matter where we live or when we were born, we are part of a generation of amateur fixers. There is at least one hardware or home improvement store in almost every community that actively promotes the "do-it-yourself" mindset. A wide array of television programs and online videos manage to convince even those of us who lack a certain manual dexterity or have little aptitude for home repairs and renovations that we should be able to tackle any project, large or small. We are assured that if we just follow a few easy steps, the finished product will be perfect. To understand the flawed premise of "do-it-yourself" marketing, one has only to stand in line at the return counter of any hardware store and look at the people with failure written all over their faces. Next to the register, there is usually a discreet display of business cards advertising professionals with the skill to fix most any botched job.

The point is that generally in life, we do not know what we do not know. Most of us have some idea of what we do know, or think we know, but we convince ourselves that we can accomplish most anything with enough effort and raw self-determination. Usually our downfall is a sense of self-reliance. When we experience failures and setbacks, we learn the hard way that we simply cannot do everything in life by ourselves. We realize that we have neither the talent nor the gifts to master even a fraction of what we might envision without the help of others.

Though this may seem counterintuitive to those who are better managers than delegators, in fact it takes a village to overcome the challenges of everyday life. When we grieve the death of one we love, we learn that grief is not a stand-alone, "do-it-yourself" experience of quick fix or self-repair. When we trust others enough to allow them to share in our grief, we open ourselves to the blessing of communal love and care.

Consider some of the ways we delegate power in our lives. If we vote in an election, we entrust our voice and civic will to those who pledge to represent us. Even when our personal opinion does not always concur with that of the majority and our preferred candidate does not prevail, good citizenship requires that we abide by the decisions made on our behalf by those representatives elected by the majority. We transfer the individual power of self to those entrusted with the greater good of our community, state, or nation.

Language is rich in reflexive pronouns. In the English language there are nine *reflexive* pronouns that are often mis-used in both spoken and written communication: myself, yourself, himself, herself, oneself, itself, ourselves, yourselves, and themselves. When used in a sentence, a reflexive pro-noun reflects back upon the subject of the sentence. Slang, social media, and online sources of news and information perpetrate modern idioms of *selfness*.

Real life teaches us that we are not sufficient unto our-selves, that our everyday lives are linked to others through the reflexive power of our collective being, "He himself is before all things, and in him all things hold together" (Co-lossians 1:17). In Scripture, the reflexive is used to empha-size the presence of God in our lives, "Now may the Lord of peace himself give you peace at all times in all ways" (2 Thessalonians 3:16). God is not a passive spectator who looks on as we struggle through life. Rather, God is an active participant in our lives, even when we make choices that allow us to experience the consequences of our own free will, "You shall know that I am the LORD your God" (Exodus 6:7).

For those who grieve, the presence of God is affirmed in the assurance of the reflexive, "And after you have suffered for a little while, the God of all grace, who has called you to his eternal glory in Christ, will himself restore, support, strengthen, and establish you" (1 Peter 5:10). God does not delegate the restoration of our soul, "he restores my soul" (Psalm 23:2). God does not assign the urgent needs of our heart and spirit to a surrogate, especially when we grieve. No other than God is at work personally in our life through the power of the Holy Spirit, "He will not let your foot be moved; he who keeps you will not slumber" (Psalm 121:3).

Though God may use others as agents for our care, God does not rely on the ingenuity of people to mitigate our grief. God alone is at the core of every spiritual transaction of comfort and grace, "Let me hear what God the LORD will speak, for he will speak peace to his people, to his faithful, to those who turn to him in their hearts" (Psalm 85:8).

And though we do not know how long our grief will last, "a little while" is not forever. We are assured that however long grief lasts, our suffering will one day be over. In the presence of God, the reflexive power of God's own self will restore, support, strengthen, and establish us, "he himself gives to all mortals life and breath and all things" (Acts 17:25).

THROUGH A
MIRROR

There is something rather extraordinary about the function of a two-way mirror—it reflects an image from one
side but is transparent on the other side. From one side, we
see only a reflection of our self, while at the same time, we
can be seen from the other side.

Our human vanity is fueled every day by media images
that suggest that a kind of artificial cosmetic beauty is a
"must have" in life. When we compare ourselves to what
is promoted as the ideal, we easily allow our sense of self to
be undermined by that which is at best only superficial. We
turn to the mirror to confirm our physical attributes, flaws,
imperfections, and deficiencies.

When we grieve, what is it that we expect to see when
we look into the two-way mirror of our soul? From one side,
we see only the bleak reality of the death of one we love.
We wonder whether there is hope for life beyond this time
of heartache and sorrow. To see what lies on the other side
of our immediate moment of grief, we must first look into
our soul. Though the mirror of the past may seem hopelessly
shattered by the heartbreak of grief, nevertheless we see
clearly the image of enduring, unbroken love.

At times of emotional and spiritual crisis, we may feel as
though we are pounding our fists against the two-way mirror

of life, silently mouthing the word *help*, desperately hoping there is someone on the other side who can read our lips and respond to our cry. Grief requires persistent prayer and the unshakeable belief that God is present, listening to every expression of our heartache. Prayer is about soul-searching honesty that has little to do with self-reproach or trumped-up guilt. Even the simplest prayer assures us of the presence of God, "When the righteous cry for help, the LORD hears, and rescues them from all their troubles" (Psalm 34:17).

When at last we break through the opaque complexities of grief, we see clearly that the two-way mirror of self-doubt and sorrow is in fact a window that is waiting only to be opened so that the presence of God may flood our soul with light.

> The Lord is the Spirit, and where the Lord's Spirit is, there is freedom. All of us are looking with unveiled faces at the glory of the Lord as if we were looking in a mirror. We are being transformed into that same image from one degree of glory to the next degree of glory. This comes from the Lord, who is the Spirit.
>
> —2 Corinthians 3:17-18 CEB

Unlike Alice in Wonderland, we have no real or imaginary ability to step through the looking glass to see what might be waiting for us on the other side of grief. Perhaps more than *what*, we should consider *who* is on the other side of the two-way mirror of our life, "'Come' my heart says, 'seek his face!' Your face, LORD, do I seek" (Psalm 27:8). When we peer into the unknown with unquestioning faith, we know with certainty that God is on the other side of the two-way mirror of our life, "At present we are looking at puzzling reflections in a mirror. The time will come when we shall see reality whole and face to face! At present all I know is a little fraction of the truth, but the time will come when I shall know it as fully as God now knows me!" (1 Corinthians 13:12-13 PHILLIPS).

On that day when we join those who have gone before us, we will stand in the presence of God and know God as fully as God now knows us. No smoke. No mirrors. Almighty, eternal God.

> Do not merely listen to the word, and so deceive yourselves. Do what it says. Anyone who listens to the word but does not do what it says is like someone who looks at his face in a mirror and, after looking at himself, goes away and immediately forgets what he looks like. But whoever looks intently into the perfect law that gives freedom, and continues in it—not forgetting what they have heard, but doing it—they will be blessed in what they do.

—James 1:22-25 NIV

COMPASSION

Whether we offer compassion or receive it, how we express compassion usually reflects our personal experience of life's most pivotal moments. Across the spectrum of compassion, there are gradations of how we experience the pain of others. As our understanding of the shades and shadows of life develops over time, the amplitude of our heart slowly grows and expands.

The word *compassion* comes from the Latin word meaning "co-suffering." How we respond to the suffering of others—with sympathy, empathy, or compassion—usually depends on whether we have had a similar experience. If we have never known the emotional devastation of all-in suffering, when one we love dies we are suddenly immersed in the tender truth of pain, "Though he brings grief, he will show compassion, so great is his unfailing love" (Lamentations 3:32 NIV). Our response to death and grief reveals how well-developed our emotional and spiritual fine motor skills really are.

Ombré is a visual effect in which hues that are in the same color family blend seamlessly from light to dark. If you have ever seen a glorious, memorable sunrise or the melting colors of a fading sunset, you have witnessed the indescribable subtleties of *ombré*. Similarly, within the range of compassion there are fine, though not always measurable nuances we use to express our care and concern for others.

Sympathy is an uncomplicated, often superficial expression of compassion. Generally, sympathy is a reaction of detached pity toward the distress or need of another. Within sympathy there may be an impulse of compassion, yet we deftly navigate around the heartbreak of another with a certain emotional detachment if we are uncomfortable with their distress. Lurking at the edge of our sympathy is sometimes a small, guilty voice that utters the silent prayer, "Thank God it's not me." Because God is unfailingly compassionate to us, we are called to greater depths of emotional and spiritual outreach well beyond mere sympathy when one we know or love is grieving, "Finally, all of you, be like-minded, be sympathetic, love one another, be compassionate and humble" (1 Peter 3:8 NIV).

Sometimes we are simply immature in our understanding of what it means to be truly compassionate. Though we may try to share in the feelings of another, through no fault of our own we are emotionally ignorant of the kind of pain that is little helped by a well-intended, though sometimes comfortless expression of sympathy, "I looked for sympathy, but there was none, for comforters, but I found none" (Psalm 69:20).

To make ourselves feel more comfortable, we may define a convenient boundary for our sympathy, "She's strong, she'll get over it." Spend some time in the greeting card aisle of any store and read a few sympathy cards if you need proof of the relatively transitory value of hollow, sometimes sugar-coated, expressions of sympathy. We may scribble a few words to personalize a poetic message in the belief that our borrowed sentiment of sympathy will somehow help the one who is suffering. In doing so, we offer only scant crumbs of care. For some, this may well be all we have or know to give. Though generally our well-intentioned sentiments are received with some appreciation, sympathy is at best a one-dimensional substitute for heartfelt compassion.

Along the *ombré* continuum of compassion, sympathy transitions to the darker hue of *empathy*. Empathy is the ability to understand the perspective of another person and share in their emotions—to feel with another. Generally we are more adept at empathy if we share a kindred perspective of life or loss or death. We express empathy when we faithfully stand alongside those who grieve through the worst of their pain and sorrow and hold their hand as they step into the unknown future. When we abandon ourselves to feel with another, we discover again that in giving, we receive—empathy fortifies our heart and augments our soul.

Perhaps the most time-honored example of true compassion is found in the parable of the good Samaritan. When asked "And who is my neighbor?" Jesus replied with this illustration,

> "A man was going down from Jerusalem to Jericho
> when he was attacked by robbers. They stripped
> him of his clothes, beat him and went away, leaving
> him half dead. A priest happened to be going down
> the same road, and when he saw the man, he passed
> by on the other side. So too, a Levite, when he came
> to the place and saw him, passed by on the other
> side. But a Samaritan, as he traveled, came where
> the man was; and when he saw him, he took pity
> on him. He went to him and bandaged his wounds,
> pouring on oil and wine. Then he put the man on
> his own donkey, brought him to an inn and took
> care of him. The next day he took out two denarii

and gave them to the innkeeper. 'Look after him,'
he said, 'and when I return, I will reimburse you for
any extra expense you may have.'
"Which of these three do you think was a neighbor
to the man who fell into the hands of robbers?"
The expert in the law replied, "The one who had
mercy on him."

—Luke 10:30-37 NIV

Whether or not we cherish religious values, the godly
compassion of the good Samaritan is still the historic gold
standard for our outreach to others, "The LORD is gracious
and righteous; our God is full of compassion" (Psalm 116:5
NIV).

Authentic *compassion* is the ability to feel into the suffering of another, well beyond the textbook definition of co-
suffering. We need only look into the fearful, traumatized
faces of immigrant children separated from their parents, or
into the anguish of a thousand other human tragedies for
our heart to be stirred with compassion, "Even in darkness
light dawns for the upright, for those who are gracious and
compassionate and righteous" (Psalm 112:4 NIV).

Whether we observe human suffering from afar or witness it in person, our first impulse is to help. We want to alle-
viate the physical and emotional pain we see and make things
better. We want to be agents of change and relief for those
who are suffering and in need, "… for the LORD your God
is gracious and compassionate" (2 Chronicles 30:9 NIV).
We offer our compassion because we ourselves have been
blessed by the compassion and presence of God, "Therefore,
as God's chosen people, holy and dearly loved, clothe yourselves with compassion, kindness, humility, gentleness and
patience" (Colossians 3:12 NIV).

When we grieve, we long for the kind of consolation that comes only from true compassion, "For the LORD comforts his people and will have compassion on his afflicted ones" (Isaiah 49:13 NIV). In the presence of God our soul finds its best comfort through the redemptive grace of compassion.

> Praise the LORD, my soul,
> and forget not all his benefits—
> who redeems your life from the pit
> and crowns you with love and compassion,
> who satisfies your desires with good things
> so that your youth is renewed like the eagle's
>
> —Psalm 103:2, 4-5 NIV

TENDER MERCY

While sitting at a lunch counter one Tuesday eating a tuna sandwich, images of a tornado in Oklahoma that caused incomprehensible destruction and loss of precious life the previous day flashed across the television screen in front of me. It is almost impossible to comprehend or visually assimilate a large-scale disaster of any kind, especially when we are not there. Somehow, it always seems more personal when it happens in a nearby state, a little closer to home. As incomplete news reports slowly solidified into factual information, human interest stories about people who survived and whose lives were devastated were also captured as part of the reporting.

Tears filled my eyes as I watched a woman with deep lacerations on her arms fearlessly picking through the rubble that was once her home. She was on a mission, determined to find her little dog despite her own need for medical attention. She was certain the dog was there somewhere— she called out, then listened. Sure enough, she heard a sound and knew the dog was alive. She tugged and pulled at a large piece of debris and finally made a hole large enough for the dog to wriggle through. The feisty Schnauzer, only a little worse for the wear, jumped into her waiting arms. There were tears and great joy for both the dog and its adoring owner.

In the face of any major disaster, there are always countless stories of tender mercy. Teachers who protect innocent children by laying down their own physical lives, and neighbors helping neighbors. The human spirit of love and kindness always prevails—it is larger than every adverse circumstance in life.

Be merciful to me, O God, be merciful to me,
for in you my soul takes refuge;
in the shadow of your wings I will take refuge,
until the destroying storms pass by.

—Psalm 57:1

Love, mercy, and grace express the very presence of God, especially when we grieve, "May mercy, peace, and love be yours in abundance" (Jude 1:2). Though these spiritual qualities are inextricably linked, mercy stands a little apart from love and grace, "Blessed are the merciful, for they will receive mercy" (Matthew 5:7). Mercy acknowledges our fundamental human need for forgiveness, "But you are a God ready to forgive, gracious and merciful, slow to anger and abounding in steadfast love" (Nehemiah 9:17). When we receive mercy from God or from others, our heart is redeemed by the grace of a love that is unearned, unmerited, and undeserved, "Be merciful, just as your Father is merciful" (Luke 6:36).

We experience the mercy of God as goodness, "The LORD is good to all: and his tender mercies are over all his works" (Psalm 145:9 KJV). We experience the mercy of God as comfort when one we love dies. "Surely goodness and mercy shall follow me all the days of my life; and I shall dwell in the house of the Lord for ever (Psalm 23:6 RSV).

We experience the mercy of God as hope, "hope in the LORD; For with the LORD there is mercy" (Psalm 130:7 KJV).

When we grieve, we commit our broken heart to the tender mercy that enfolds us in the presence of God.

By the tender mercy of our God,
the dawn from on high will break upon us,
to give light to those who sit in darkness and in the
shadow of death,
to guide our feet into the way of peace.

—Luke 1:78-79

CONDUIT

All streams run to the sea,
but the sea is not full;
to the place where the streams flow,
there they continue to flow.

—Ecclesiastes 1:7

A friend received a property survey for a new home he was buying which required his approval before the transaction could be finalized. To his surprise, the survey showed a city easement for a large conduit pipe situated some forty feet directly under the house—the oversized kind you see rumbling down the highway strapped to the back of an eighteen-wheel flatbed truck. This particular conduit serves as a kind of urban aqueduct. It carries excess water from a major expressway to a nearby creek system which in turn flows into a municipal waterway large enough to manage the run-off.

There is a significant difference between the function of an ordinary pipe that brings water into a home or building, and a conduit that uses gravitational force to direct the flow of large amounts of water. As we direct the continuum of service, flow, and outlet that runs throughout our experience of grief, so we direct the course of our grief. Though our emotions may range from trickle to torrent from one day to the next, conduits direct us forward as we change and grow beyond our grief. There are no dead-end conduits—we are always becoming.

When we grieve, we depend for a while on the steady drip, drip, drip of a reliable pipeline—flowers that lift our spirit, notes of condolence that comfort our heart, spontaneous expressions of care offered by friends and family. As others step away from our grief and resume the rhythm of their own daily lives, we are easily overwhelmed by fear, anxiety, and worry. We pray for the comfort and assurance that only a reliable spiritual conduit can provide.

> Therefore let all who are faithful
> offer prayer to you;
> at a time of distress, the rush of mighty waters
> shall not reach them.

—Psalm 32:6

The presence of God is the conduit that directs our despair and hopelessness beyond all present and future uncertainty toward the outlet that is new life, "The water that I will give will become in them a spring of water gushing up to eternal life" (John 4:14).

There are those we know and love who supply our pipeline, and those God calls to serve as conduits of God's presence. Human conduits come in only one size—love, "Many waters cannot quench love, neither can floods drown it" (Song of Solomon 8:7). Conduits are those who direct us to a local grief support group where we can share our story with others. Conduits lead us away from the dailiness of our grief. Conduits continually assure us that we are useful, that we have something to offer to the world, and that our experience of life and death can inspire and encourage others. Conduits do not push us to abandon our grief. Conduits give us space and personal latitude until we are ready to engage in pursuits that will reenergize our life in ways that feel normal, good, and productive. Conduits: experts in fluid grief and liquid love.

As survivors of death and grief, we are called to be conduits of the presence of God to future generations. We direct those we love not to the run-off of grief, but toward the flow-through of faith, "The words of the mouth are deep waters; the fountain of wisdom is a gushing stream" (Proverbs 18:4). As conduits, we lead those we love to the source of living water found only in the presence of God, "Keep your heart with all vigilance, for from it flow the springs of life" (Proverbs 4:23).

WAITING

In the liminal time between the death of one we love and our reawakening to fullness of life, there is a vast expanse of waiting. In an article entitled "Grieving as Sacred Space," Richard Rohr defines *liminal time* in this way:

> ...when you have left the "tried and true" but have not yet been able to replace it with anything else. . . It is when you are in between your old comfort zone and any possible new answer . . . If you are not trained in how to hold anxiety, how to live with ambiguity, how to entrust and wait—you will run . . . Anything to flee from this terrible "cloud of unknowing."[8]

Waiting is counterintuitive to human nature, especially in our instant-gratification culture of the twenty-first century. We are experts at *doing* and remarkably inept at *waiting*. Waiting defies our ingrained need to be measurably productive doing something—anything—all the time. More often than not, waiting is a frustrating state of inactivity that challenges our heart and tests our spiritual fortitude.

> The LORD is good to those who wait for him,
> to the soul that seeks him.
> It is good that one should wait quietly
> for the salvation of the LORD.

—Lamentations 3:25-26

One of the settings in which we see or experience a liminal time of waiting is in a medical or hospital environment. Whether we wait in a physician's office for a diagnosis or the results of testing, or we pace the anonymous halls with anxious worry about a loved one who is in surgery, waiting is the silent backdrop of every action and interaction that is part of health and healing. At any time, there is always someone waiting—one who waits for birth, one who waits for treatment, one who waits for death, one who waits on bended knee desperately praying for the recovery of a loved one, "But it is for you, O LORD, that I wait; it is you, O Lord my God, who will answer" (Psalm 38:15). When we look into the faces of those who wait, we see lives torn between hope and despair, "Wait for the LORD; be strong, and let your heart take courage; wait for the LORD!" (Psalm 27:14).

Waiting is one of the unexpected disciplines of grief that in the moment can seem harsh or even punitive, "What is my strength, that I should wait? And what is my end, that I should be patient?" (Job 6:11). Part of waiting is an unfamiliar inertia that gives our heart space to assimilate grief in slow-motion. And in the liminal time of waiting that is grief, we find the solitude and silence that allow us to look within, "You desire truth in the inward being; therefore teach me wisdom in my secret heart" (Psalm 51:6). We pray, meditate, and notice the presence of God in us and around us, "I wait for the LORD, my soul waits, and in his word I hope" (Psalm 130:5).

When life as we know it is abruptly brought to a halt by the finality of death, our hopes and dreams are shaken— the future we envisioned as certainty suddenly is no more. Though some of our assumptions about the future may survive the death of one we love, all prior aspirations and expectations become more of a commentary on our past. In the liminal time of waiting for life to be better, our perspective slowly shifts, "Lead me in your truth, and teach me, for you are the God of my salvation; for you I wait all day long" (Psalm 25:5). We begin to see that today is the future we believed in yesterday, "He has made everything suitable for its time; moreover he has put a sense of past and future into their minds, yet they cannot find out what God has done from the beginning to the end" (Ecclesiastes 3:11). To capture a glimpse of the future is to give the world a second chance, "Surely there is a future, and your hope will not be cut off" (Proverbs 23:18). God waits while we wait.

> Therefore the LORD waits to be gracious to you;
> therefore he will rise up to show mercy to you.
> For the LORD is a God of justice;
> blessed are all those who wait for him.
> —Isaiah 30:18

Whether we wait for twenty-four hours, for days, for weeks, for months, or even for years, when we live into a liminal time of waiting we move slowly away from the threshold of grief, "'For I know the plans I have for you,' declares the LORD, 'plans to prosper you and not to harm you, plans to give you hope and a future'" (Jeremiah 29:11 NIV). We claim our future in the life that really is life through the presence of God, "the same yesterday, today, and forever" (Hebrews 13:8).

> They are to do good, to be rich in good works,
> generous, and ready to share, thus storing up for
> themselves the treasure of a good foundation for the
> future, so that they may take hold of the life that
> really is life.
> —1 Timothy 6:18-20

DON'T MISS
THE SPRING

At any time of unprecedented crisis when the entire world is single-minded in its focus on the prevention and containment of pandemic disease, the daunting challenges of contagion stretch healthcare resources and test the professional fortitude of hospitals, businesses, and individuals. During extraordinary times, our innate survival instinct urges us to shop, stock up, and hoard so that we have enough supplies if not for the duration, then at least for a while.

Amid worldwide chaos caused by an unpredictable pathogen, there is helplessness, fear, and anxiety. As those who have experienced the death of a loved one know too well, loss of control is an inescapable dimension of grief that easily distracts us from the sum and substance of ordinary daily living.

From the day my husband received a terminal diagnosis, I was oblivious to almost everything in life except the dire dailiness of our race against death. A few months after he died, an acquaintance asked me about some event that happened during the three months of his illness. Without much thought, I quickly answered, "Oh, I missed the spring that year." In truth, I have little recollection of anything during that time except coming and going from the hospital each day and my inner struggle to reconcile my faith with medical reality.

During the worst of times, the changing seasons remind us of the steady, faithful presence of God, "for now the winter is past, the rain is over and gone" (Song of Solomon 2:11). In spring, there is unexpected comfort in the beauty of nature and the promise of new life—the first daffodils emerging from the earth, the rich colors of tulips in bloom, the first tentative azaleas in bud. Almost overnight, trees seem to burst into full leaf. As surely as the first suggestions of spring fade, nature inevitably moves toward the heat of summer, the first chill of autumn, and the cold of winter. So too, dire global events run their course and life again moves forward in new, unexpected ways.

In the meantime, we wait—for a cure, for a vaccine, or for some resolution to whatever momentary crisis brings life to a standstill. When the entire world grinds slowly to a halt, there is a once-in-a-lifetime opportunity to push both the pause and reset buttons of life simultaneously. At the same time that we are forced to adjust our desire to go, do, and participate fully in the diversions and distractions of the world, we are also compelled by circumstance to be fully present to issues of survival in the here and now. For those who grieve, we may be able to reframe our experience of personal loss in the context of an international event.

How we live through a rare moment of uncertainty and waiting is a choice. In an unfamiliar time of disorder and inactivity we can live in frustration or we can use the experience as an opportunity to explore and embrace that which enriches our soul and grows our faith. If we fully enter into an unexpected meantime, we have space for reflection and introspection. We learn through circumstances beyond our control more about who we are at the core of our being.

As we anxiously wait to resume the normal rhythm of our life, we can pray for each person who is affected by illness and for the stamina and strength of hospital workers and caregivers who selflessly serve on the frontline of health-care to overcome stealth disease. We can pray intentionally, by name, for all those who grieve. We can pray for the those who work to develop treatments and a cure for devastating infections.

We can use our time for physical and spiritual self-care. We can use our time to care for others in person or remotely. We can use our time to build deeper family relationships. We can abandon petty squabbles and tired estrangements. We can be present to the world with love, compassion, and forgiveness.

As each global crisis slowly shifts and nears an end, the world begins to relax. Before we can advance, there are questions each of us should answer about what we have learned:

– Have I enlarged my mind?

– Have I expanded my heart?

– Have I grown in my spirit?

– Have I nurtured my soul?

Much like the spring, life going forward will be more beautiful than ever before. Those who persevere through a time of great physical, personal, and economic stress at last prevail through the grace and presence of God.

For the mountains may depart
and the hills be removed,

but my steadfast love shall not depart from you,
and my covenant of peace shall not be removed,
says the LORD, who has compassion on you.

—Isaiah 54:10

A LEVEL PATH

An urban trail in Dallas which runs through one of the most densely developed sections of the city follows the path of an old railroad line that once went through the nearby downtown area. The distance from endpoint to endpoint is 3.5 miles. Because the beautifully landscaped trail is generally straight with only a few slight turns along the way, it is ideal for walking, running, inline skating, and cycling. Perhaps its most rewarding feature for both serious and casual exercise enthusiasts is that the surface is level.

We spend most of our life at a level place of daily existence. Whether we live in a state of chronic disarray or in pursuit of elusive perfection, we rely on the predictable dailiness of our ordinary routine. Even when life seems more about controlled chaos than order, we know where we live and conform ourselves to whatever conditions our environment might suggest. Generally, we are good at being adaptable.

When the death of one we love turns our life wrong side out, our dependable, level path suddenly becomes a treacherous, rocky road. When we feel pressed by others or by our life's circumstances to navigate grief quickly, we may stumble and miss the lessons of grief along the way, "Teach me your way, O LORD, and lead me on a level path" (Psalm 27:11).

Our natural assumption is that the path leads somewhere, even if it is simply to the end and back. Similarly, grief is an emotional round trip that leads us to a place where we en-counter our inmost self, "The way of the righteous is level; O Just One, you make smooth the path of the righteous" (Isaiah 26:7). Along the way, we discover more about who we are and where we are in life, "You show me the path of life; in your presence there is fullness of joy" (Psalm 16:11). As we return to life, we follow a new level path that leads us toward the future, "Keep straight the path of your feet, and all your ways will be sure" (Proverbs 4:26).

Over the course of any trail, there are places to get on and off. There are designated areas with water, benches, and shade trees that allow us to pause and refresh before resum-ing the trail. We learn the enduring truths of grief when we observe the distance markers and stop to rest along the way.

– We learn that it takes courage and faith to walk into the darkness of the unknown future. What-ever our conviction of faith or our place of trust, we may discern the voice of God as we journey through grief, "And when you turn to the right or when you turn to the left, your ears shall hear a word behind you, saying, 'This is the way; walk in it'" (Isaiah 30:21). God lights our way out of the darkness and shows us the level path, "Your word is a lamp to my feet and a light to my path" (Psalm 119:105).

– We learn that God meets us in the depths of our soul when we grieve, "for you are with me; your rod and your staff—they comfort me" (Psalm 23:4). God leads us toward the path of new life, "He leads me in right paths for his name's sake" (Psalm 23:3).

– We learn that submitting our will to the will of God leads us to a level path for life in the present—here and now, "Teach me to do your will, for you are my God. Let your good spirit lead me on a level path" (Psalm 143:10). Seeking and finding the will of God for our life is one of the most teachable moments of faith, "And the world and its desire are passing away, but those who do the will of God live forever" (1 John 2:17). If we abandon our sense of self-determination and our desire to control, we are assured that God will show us the way, "Make me to know your ways, O Lord; teach me your paths" (Psalm 25:4).

The path of grief requires a certain fundamental belief that one day, life will be better. When we move forward in faith and leave the past behind, the presence of God leads us toward the level path that is our God-appointed future, "All the paths of the Lord are steadfast love and faithfulness" (Psalm 25:10).

RECONCILIATION

Though for some it is a thankless task, from time to time most of us make the effort to reconcile our finances. We balance the checkbook, enter transactions into a bookkeeping program, or look at our records and statements to determine whether we have enough money now and for the future. For those who choose to defer or entirely avoid the necessity of periodic financial accounting, the consequences can be dire. When we spend more than we earn, we set ourselves up for a life that constantly teeters on the edge of financial disaster. The result of responsible financial behavior is that one day we are able to realize our dreams and long-term goals—home ownership, travel, college education, a comfortable retirement. We accomplish our objectives and achieve our goals through the consistent discipline of financial reconciliation.

Because reconciling ourselves to the death of one we love is a continuous process of adjustment and acceptance, it is one of the most arduous challenges of grief. Before we can move forward, grief compels us to reconcile the balance of our life, though seldom is this a straight-line operation. First, we weigh our need for a new mindset and new life skills through soul-searching and introspection. Next, we broaden our horizon to include possibilities we may have never dared to imagine. Finally, we reconcile ourselves to what may be an altered, possibly unfamiliar place for us in the world as we look forward to the future.

Reconciliation is a slow progression that is generally erratic, sometimes perplexing, and at times frustrating. To reconcile the magnitude of our loss and resolve some of the more complicated, conflicting emotions of grief, we may need the perspective and expertise of a professional. A compassionate, concerned listener may be able to suggest a context that gives us direction and leads us toward personal reconciliation.

Forgiveness is an integral part of personal reconciliation, "One who forgives an affront fosters friendship, but one who dwells on disputes will alienate a friend" (Proverbs 17:9). We may need to ask for forgiveness, "To the Lord our God belong mercy and forgiveness" (Daniel 9:9). We may need to forgive ourselves, "Whenever you stand praying, forgive, if you have anything against anyone" (Mark 11:25).

An outcome of personal reconciliation is that we emerge from grief with a greater awareness of humanity—our own and that of others, "You shall love your neighbor as yourself" (Mark 12:31). Because of our experience of death and grief, we are more attuned to the needs and suffering of innocent, unsuspecting victims of every kind in every place. We are quick to disavow expressions of racism, discrimination, and bigotry. We respond with solidarity and compassion to those who feel marginalized in a world where recurring violence, public outrage, and protest are more the norm than the exception. Through our personal experience of loss and suffering, we become more sensitive human beings better attuned to the needs of humanity.

Reconciliation is about our spiritual alignment with God. When our heart beats with the heartbeat of God, we move away from grief to live with expectation and hope,

"For you, O Lord, are my hope, my trust, O LORD, from my youth" (Psalm 71:5). When our soul is at one with God, we reconcile ourselves to God's perfect plan and God's perfect timing in our life, "Your kingdom come. Your will be done, on earth as it is in heaven" (Matthew 6:1).

The presence of God at work in our lives may lead us into the future in unexpected ways, not despite of the death of one we love, but because of the death of one we love, "All this is from God, who reconciled us to himself through Christ, and has given us the ministry of reconciliation" (2 Corinthians 5:18). When our accounts with God are balanced down to the last penny of our spiritual capital, we are blessed with the peace of reconciliation found only in the presence of God, "Peace I leave with you; my peace I give to you. I do not give to you as the world gives. Do not let your hearts be troubled, and do not let them be afraid" (John 14:27).

LIVING WATER

On a Monday morning at zero dark thirty, the building manager sent an urgent message to all residents informing us that there was a break in the water main to the building, and that there would be no water service, possibly for several hours. In my unit, there was still enough pressure and hot water in the tank to have a tepid shower before escaping to my office, where there was both running water and plumbing that worked.

I had invited guests to my home for the evening and debated whether or not to cancel. As the day progressed, there were periodic updates—each report seemed more dire than the last. This was not a surprise, given the age of the infrastructure in most large cities. In addition to the original leak, workers found a large boulder that hindered their access to a second leak. And so it went throughout the day. I warned my guests in advance that there might not be any running water, but we decided to have our get-together as planned.

They came and left, but still there was no running water. I cleared the table and tried not to obsess over dirty dishes in the sink. Outside the window, my bedtime lullaby was the insistent noise of a compressor that generated sufficient light for work to continue through the night. As is usually the case with perseverance and a lot of hard work, the leak was fixed, the water main repaired, and in the morning the water supply and pressure were back to normal. Though I had allowed this temporary inconvenience to take on larger-than-life proportions in my mind, it caused me to pause and consider the significance of running water as a metaphor for that which is really important in life.

As I stood at the kitchen sink the next morning washing dishes from the night before, I thought about how dependent we are on running water. I thought about all the appliances and modern conveniences that cannot function without running water and how much we take this blessing for granted, especially in developed countries. My mind wandered to those in other parts of the world whose daily job it is to carry water great distances, sometimes from contaminated sources, and to all those who have no access to water suitable for drinking or bathing or washing.

> O God, you are my God, I seek you,
> my soul thirsts for you;
> my flesh faints for you,
> as in a dry and weary land where there is no water.
> —Psalm 63:1

Running water is dynamic; it is alive with possibilities. It comes from somewhere and goes toward something. It may ebb and flow, but it is never static. If it is dammed or obstructed, it may stagnate and provide an incubator for bacteria and parasites that can cause serious health conditions. When we grieve, we may sense a heavy stillness that feels like spiritual stagnation. After the death of one we love, we may feel powerless to remove the emotional and spiritual obstacles that block the flow of life. The presence of God is the life force that restores the course of living water that inevitably runs toward new life, "You visit the earth and water it, you greatly enrich it; the river of God is full of water" (Psalm 65:9).

We know how water feels when it slips through our fingers. We feel its force when we wade into the ocean and feel the changing tide. We know how water sounds, yet we cannot describe the noise of a slow, steady drip or that of an overwhelming flood. When we grieve, our senses are saturated by the indescribable certainty that the presence of God is the living water that flows through our experience of grief, "As the scripture has said, 'Out of the believer's heart shall flow rivers of living water'" (John 7:38).

Even as water creates a reflection when there is light, we reflect the presence of God when we extend the gift of living water to others, "Just as water reflects the face, so one human heart reflects another" (Proverbs 27:19). Grief is about giving and receiving the water of life that flows far deeper than any mere surface reflection, "A generous person will be enriched, and one who gives water will get water" (Proverbs 11:25). Only living water can satisfy the thirst of our soul for the presence of God, "'If you knew the gift of God, and who it is that is saying to you, "Give me a drink," you would have asked him, and he would have given you living water'" (John 4:10).

> God is our refuge and strength,
> a very present help in trouble.
> Therefore we will not fear, though the earth
> should change,
> though the mountains shake in the heart of the sea;
> though its waters roar and foam,
> though the mountains tremble with its tumult.
>
> —Psalm 46:1-3

SEEING EYES

On a rainy afternoon in December, I attended the funeral of a woman whose husband I knew and wanted to support in his grief. He was an adoring, loving spouse, in every way a faithful servant who cared for his wife throughout her long decline into Alzheimer's disease. The service was a fitting tribute to a joyful life, a life that was well-lived in love and service to her family, her church, and others.

As I entered the building fussing with a wet umbrella, I noticed a perfectly groomed, well-dressed woman sitting on a nearby sofa with a service dog at her feet. She was in every way normal, and she was totally blind. I spoke briefly to the minister, tucked away my rain gear, and found a seat on a back row of the sanctuary, which was adorned for Christmas with a bright array of seasonal poinsettias.

As I looked around the room, I noticed the woman seated directly across the aisle. I observed her throughout the service as she sang the hymns and participated in the order of worship. What caught my attention, though, was her service dog—a beautiful black Labrador mix with dark, no-nonsense eyes. Clearly, theirs was a strong partnership of complete trust and mutual dependence.

As the dog settled in for the service, he stretched out at her feet on the cool tile floor. Though he seemed to be resting, he was constantly scanning the people around her. I smiled at the dog, hoping to assure him that I was friend rather than foe. In response, there was not so much as a thump of his tail to acknowledge my well-intentioned overture. The dog was all business—he was perfectly trained to do his job, and he was at work.

The dog wore not only a leather lead harness but also a choke collar with a leash. There was a natural rhythm to the communication between him and his mistress. As he responded to her non-verbal directions, his every move demonstrated that he was highly trained to be the eyes of his companion. When she moved, he stirred, when he got up, she gripped the leash and gently pulled the collar to affirm her authority and presence.

Sometime later, I began to think more about the dog— about the patient hands and voices who trained him to be the eyes of one without sight, about his devotion and loyalty to his mistress, about his responsibility to ensure her safety, and about his own care and well-being. I thought about his life of duty and service, a life of complete obedience dedicated solely to the privilege of caring for one in need. I wondered whether he enjoyed some time to play and run for a while each day without a harness, a collar, or a leash. I thought about whether he understood—by instinct or by training— that his purpose in life was to be a faithful caregiver.

As I sat there, I closed my eyes for a few moments and tried to imagine what it would be like to navigate life without the precious gift of eyesight, to be entirely dependent not only on the kindness of others, but also on a dog—a living being that could neither speak nor respond other than by training and intuitive compassion.

I will lead the blind
by a road they do not know,
by paths they have not known
I will guide them.
I will turn the darkness before them into light,
the rough places into level ground.
These are the things I will do,
and I will not forsake them.

—Isaiah 42:16

In the darkness of these thoughts, I grasped anew the power of faith and trust in the absolute presence of God, "You're blessed when you get your inside world—your mind and heart—put right. Then you can see God in the outside world" (Matthew 5:8 MSG).

Think about what it would be like to take off the harness, collar, and leash of sadness and sorrow that constrain us when we grieve. Think about what it would be like to abandon ourselves to complete dependence on God to guide us, give us sure direction, and lead us when we are too blind to believe in the future, or too debilitated by grief to hope, "so that, with the eyes of your heart enlightened, you may know what is the hope to which he has called you, what are the riches of his glorious inheritance among the saints" (Ephesians 1:18). May the eyes of our heart be so enlightened that we feel the hand of God in ours, "though we stumble, we shall not fall headlong, for the LORD holds us by the hand" (Psalm 37:24).

Though we cannot see the presence of God, we believe in faith that God never leaves our side, that God is with us every step of the way. May we live with open eyes, with seeking eyes, with seeing eyes, for through the presence of God the blindness of our grief is healed, "the LORD opens the eyes of the blind. The LORD lifts up those who are bowed down; the LORD loves the righteous" (Psalm 146:8).

RESTORE MY SOUL

After a prolonged period of analysis, evaluation, and discussion, a challenging business matter was finally concluded. When an announcement was made a few days later, it was not the one that had been widely expected. Only then did I fully appreciate the mental, emotional, and physical energy our team had invested during long months of work on the project. I realized, too, that I felt drained, that my personal reserves were completely spent. My first prayer was that God would restore my soul. My second prayer was that God would renew my strength. I needed rest, not only for my body, but also for my mind and spirit.

It is humanly impossible to isolate a single part of our being and designate it for restoration without equal attention to other aspects of self that are inevitably affected by stress, fatigue, and exhaustion. The experience of grief vividly illustrates this singular quality of human nature. When our resources are depleted by circumstance, our body, mind, heart, and spirit long for restoration, "O Lord, by these things people live, and in all these is the life of my spirit. Oh, restore me to health and make me live" (Isaiah 38:16)!

An *ambiguous illusion* is an image that has "two pictures in one." It is a tool sometimes used in psychology to test perception and interpretation. At first, the viewer may see only one image, but after some time or a shift in focus, the viewer is able to see the second picture.

The word *restore* is a kind of ambiguous illusion. For within the word *restore* we find two possibilities. For any real experience of restoration, the first prerequisite is that we rest.

I keep the Lord always before me;
because he is at my right hand, I shall not be
moved.
Therefore my heart is glad, and my soul rejoices;
my body also rests secure.

—Psalm 16:8-9

We rest when we take time to care for ourselves physically. We rest when we shut out the noise of the world—the insistent blare of the radio or television or the more subtle, excited noise of social media. More difficult to control is our own internal noise—the circular conversation of our mind that seems to have no *off* switch. Noise from without or within agitates our spirit, roils our mind, and distracts us from physical and mental restoration, "For God alone my soul waits in silence, for my hope is from him" (Psalm 62:5).

A different, perhaps bolder image found within the ambiguous illusion of the word *restore* is that of being restored, "He restores my soul" (Psalm 23:3) or "He renews my strength" (NLT). Our intuitive need for restoration usually comes from a sense of personal emptiness. The shelves of that place deep inside us that stock the inventory of our emotional and spiritual substance feel bare because we have given away or used up most of the resources that enable us to give without limitation. When we are emptied by the demands of life without pausing to be replenished, we pray that God will re-store our life with a fresh stock of personal capital, not to hoard or keep for ourselves, but to give away freely, without reservation, "Return, O my soul, to your rest, for the LORD has dealt bountifully with you" (Psalm 116:7).

When we grieve, for a while our emotional and spiritual capacity is diminished. Grief can bring us to our knees as we concede our helplessness and complete dependence on the grace of God, "My grace is sufficient for you, for power is made perfect in weakness" (2 Corinthians 12:9). And though we may not entirely recover from the death of one we love, inevitably our energy and sense of self are restored, "Restore us to yourself, O LORD, that we may be restored; renew our days as of old" (Lamentations 5:21). The presence of God replenishes the storehouse of our soul with a limitless supply of all that is imperishable, "the fruit of the Spirit is love, joy, peace, patience, kindness, generosity, faithfulness, gentleness, and self-control" (Galatians 5:22).

THE PENNY

As I returned to my car from a quick stop at the drug store, I happened to look down at the pavement and saw a penny. Though it was dirty, scratched, and almost unrecognizable as a coin, I picked it up and put it with the other change in my wallet.

After my husband died, I seemed to find pennies everywhere, sometimes in the most unusual and unexpected places. Each discovery felt like a sign of his continuing presence to me. Though the notion was surely a little irrational, at the time it was very real to me. In retrospect, I realize that I was grasping for anything that represented a tangible connection to his spirit. From time to time, I still find the odd penny at moments when I need some emotional reassurance. It happened recently at the car wash on a day when my spirit was longing for his loving presence.

When one we love dies, most of us hang on to anything and everything that has the potential to keep us connected to his or her abiding spirit. When we pick up a sweater or a well-worn piece of clothing that belonged to our loved one, usually the first thing we do is bury our nose in the fabric to smell for the familiar scent which assures us that our life together was real. We seek an invisible presence through visible reminders of their life. The deep longing of our inmost soul is to know that though they are now unseen, our loved one is still present to us, "Your way was through the sea, your path, through the mighty waters; yet your footprints were unseen" (Psalm 77:19).

We feel the abiding presence of the one we love and now grieve in unmistakable moments of whispered love. We sense their nearness in the soothing calm of a gentle breeze or the quiet laughter of a burbling stream. We glimpse their reflection when we rest beside still waters. We delight in their enduring presence through our children and grandchildren and all those who inherit the lasting legacy of the one we love and now grieve.

Grief and death take the true measure of our faith. Because we believe in that which is unseen and eternal, we are assured that the immortal soul of our loved one lives on after death.

> When this perishable body puts on imperishability,
> and this mortal body puts on immortality, then the
> saying that is written will be fulfilled:
> "Death has been swallowed up in victory."
> "Where, O death, is your victory?
> Where, O death, is your sting?"
> —1 Corinthians 15:54-55

In the conviction of our faith, we know that the bond of enduring love we shared with our loved one here on earth cannot be shattered or broken by death, "Although you have not seen him, you love him; and even though you do not see him now, you believe in him and rejoice with an indescribable and glorious joy, for you are receiving the outcome of your faith" (1 Peter 1:8-9).

We cherish each sign and suggestion that intimates the abiding spiritual presence of our loved one to us on this side of heaven. Though for a while we are separated in body, we know that one day we will be reunited in fullness of joy, "Have you believed because you have seen me? Blessed are those who have not seen and yet have come to believe" (John 20:29). In the presence of God, we honor all that is invisible, "To the King of the ages, immortal, invisible, the only God, be honor and glory forever and ever. Amen" (1 Timothy 1:17).

> So we do not lose heart. Though our outer nature is wasting away, our inner nature is being renewed every day. For this slight momentary affliction is preparing for us an eternal weight of glory beyond all comparison, because we look not to the things that are seen but to the things that are unseen; for the things that are seen are transient, but the things that are unseen are eternal.

—2 Corinthians 4:16-18 RSV

CENTER CUT

One morning on the way to the office I stopped at a local deli to get a sandwich for lunch. They make the best brownies in town, so I added one to my order. The counter clerk smiled and picked out what she called a "center cut" brownie, one from the middle of the pan, a perfect square with no crusty edges. She said with a knowing smile, "Beef and brownies—both should be center cuts."

As I walked out the door, I laughed over this creative turn of phrase. Whether or not we are carnivores or brownie lovers, many of us are indeed "center cut" kind of people—sometimes only the best part of the whole will do. Later, as I tucked into the brownie I began to think about what constitutes the "center cut" in our lives. What do we value? What is the real substance of our life? What is the highest and best to which we aspire in life?

> While Jesus and his disciples were traveling, Jesus entered a village where a woman named Martha welcomed him as a guest. She had a sister named Mary, who sat at the Lord's feet and listened to his message. By contrast, Martha was preoccupied with getting everything ready for their meal. So Martha came to him and said, "Lord, don't you care that my sister has left me to prepare the table all by myself? Tell her to help me."

The Lord answered, "Martha, Martha, you are worried and distracted by many things. One thing is necessary. Mary has chosen the better part. It won't be taken away from her."

—Luke 10:38-42 CEB

Many of us have been caregivers or nursed those we love who have died. Like Martha, we are experts at doing. Martha had the gift of hospitality and graciously welcomed guests into her home. Her self-appointed task that day was preparing a meal for her family and a beloved friend. She was doing it with love and great care and wanted it to be perfect.

Her sister Mary wanted nothing more than to enjoy an enriching visit with their company. One translation says that she settled in to listen to what Jesus had to say. Clearly, Martha felt put upon by her sister's unwillingness to share the workload. She considered Jesus a close enough friend to complain and ask him to compel Mary to help her. In the spirit of love and friendship, Jesus gently chided Martha and pointed out that she was preoccupied and distracted by setting the table and other preparations for the meal to come. Jesus went on to point out that those things were not really important.

And then he got to the "center cut" moment of their conversation, "Mary has chosen the better part." In other words, Mary chose to immerse herself in the substance of the visit, listening to Jesus, soaking in his love, his wisdom, and his presence. The lesson is that the important things in life cannot be taken away from us—not by life or death or crisis or the routine tasks that distract us and cause us to wander away from the presence of God, "Because your steadfast love is better than life, my lips will praise you" (Psalm 63:3).

When we grieve, we are forced to examine the "center cut" of our life. For perhaps the first time in life, we understand what really matters and find that most of what we once thought was important is transitory and lacks real spiritual value. Grief causes us to go deep within our soul to find not only the resources necessary for our survival, but also to find the center cut, the better part, the presence of God.

> They will hunger no more, and thirst no more;
> the sun will not strike them,
> nor any scorching heat;
> for the Lamb at the center of the throne will be
> their shepherd,
> and he will guide them to springs of the water of life,
> and God will wipe away every tear from their eyes.

—Revelation 7:16-17

THOUSAND-
PERSON ARMY

When we take ourselves out of the crosshairs of daily life and gradually begin to focus again on life going on around us, this is a sure sign that we are making progress in grief. We see things differently and appreciate the beauty of nature in a different, more spiritual way. We consider the world and acknowledge that we are part of a continuum of sorrow and joy, disappointment and hope, loss and victory, death and life. We better understand the heart and mind of God because we have grieved.

A few years ago I attended a college graduation at the quasi-military institution my beloved father attended. As a proud member of the corps of cadet, upon graduation in 1941 he was commissioned as a second lieutenant in the United States Army and immediately deployed to serve in World War II. Over the graduation weekend, I saw cadets on campus enjoying their proud tradition and felt my father's warm presence around every corner. Amid the noise and celebration of a new generation of graduates, I experienced a private reunion of love and remembrance with my father.

Gratitude is an aspect of grief that seems oddly counter-intuitive to our experience of loss. Who is ever really grateful for being forced by death to experience grief? Yet when we reflect on those who have been present to us in our time of pain and sorrow, we see that we have been supported by a thousand-person army. We give thanks for the physical and spiritual presence of those who love us when we are heartbroken and truly comfortless. We give thanks for those who are tireless in meeting our most mundane daily needs through a time of deep grief. We give thanks for those who are faithful in their prayers for our restoration to life. Gratitude is an endowment of grief that enlarges our soul and our spirit. Inevitably, the death of one we love leads us to a deeper appreciation of life, "O give thanks to the LORD, for he is good; for his steadfast love endures forever" (1 Chronicles 16:34).

Author Wayne Muller writes,

> It is impossible to create a sufficient, contented life by ourselves. In truth, we do nothing at all completely by ourselves. We absolutely depend on a living community of countless others who accompany us each step of our lives. Have we ever grown all our own food, built our own homes, woven cloth for our own clothing, or produced our own electricity? Every moment we live, it is through the generous labor of countless lives.[9]

Among the thousand-person army that marches through our lives each day are countless nameless people who acknowledge us with a smile or a gesture of personal outreach. We are blessed by those who do the immeasurably valuable though sometimes thankless work of the world—childcare professionals, teachers, mentors, grocery clerks, bus drivers, school crossing guards, fire fighters, law enforcement officers, dry cleaners, hospitality workers, housekeepers, service professionals, nursing home aides, sitters, pharmacists, dentists, and the countless dedicated doctors and nurses who work tirelessly to save lives every day.

If we stop to count those who attend to the needs of our lives, the number easily climbs into the thousands. Well beyond salary or status, these people share one thing in common—a single-minded commitment to service, "Serve wholeheartedly, as if you were serving the Lord" (Ephesians 6:7 NIV). Service to others is an expression of human grace that inhales gratitude and exhales love. Service to others transcends grief. Service to others heals our heart and renews our spirit. Service to others demonstrates the power and presence of God at work in the world.

How do we serve others as an expression of gratitude? Perhaps we lead or attend a grief group and offer a listening, compassionate heart as we care for others and for ourselves. Perhaps we join a nonprofit group that supports a cause, one that feels especially personal because of our experience of the death of one we love. Perhaps we volunteer and offer pro bono professional services to improve the lives of others. Our response may be, "But I am not a leader or a world changer." It is not necessary to be either, "Each of you should use whatever gift you have received to serve others, as faithful stewards of God's grace in its various forms" (1 Peter 4:10 NIV). In the words of the Greek philosopher Archimedes, "Give me a place to stand, and a lever long enough, and I will move the world."

The gratitude of grief inspires us be instruments of love and change in the world, "For God is not unjust; he will not overlook your work and the love that you showed for his sake in serving the saints, as you still do" (Hebrews 6:10). When we enlist in the thousand-person army and join the legion of those who serve others, we stand ready to change lives and the world.

In the aftermath of contemporary incidents of racial discrimination, violence, and senseless death, the best hope for a real, lasting social transformation—beyond the obvious need for a sea change in the historic disparity between those divided by issues of race—is that we must all be better and do better—together, now. Change starts with learning how to be truly colorblind as a society even as we embrace the gifts of our diversity. We must teach our children both by what we say and how we act and live, "But the aim of such instruction is love that comes from a pure heart, a good conscience, and sincere faith" (1 Timothy 1:5).

We must be unfailingly polite, whether in person or on social media. We must model kindness, civility, and respect for all people everywhere—everyone, no exceptions—especially those who look different from the person we see in our own mirror.

> He has told you, O mortal, what is good;
> and what does the LORD require of you
> but to do justice, and to love kindness,
> and to walk humbly with your God?
> —Micah 6:8

We must be loving, act with love, and practice absolute love, "I act with steadfast love, justice, and righteousness in the earth, for in these things I delight, says the LORD" (Jeremiah 9:24). We must change or unlearn our generational conditioning and habits of thinking and doing until at last our love for each and every living human being conquers hate and overcomes evil in the world.

When we are present to others with gratitude, love, and service, we express with our hands and heart the presence of God to each person in the thousand-person army, "Serve the LORD with celebration!" (Psalm 100:2 CEB).

WHOLE LIFE

B efore my husband died in the early hours of a hot July night, there was a bright, shining moment of sheer silence in which the power of God was unmistakably present in that dim, close hospital room. Leighton gripped my hand for a few long seconds then suddenly relaxed as God freed his soul from his worn-out body. When at last my beloved took his final labored breath two hours later, I felt alone and strangely abandoned—by him and by God.

During my husband's ninety-day illness, I experienced the extremes of hope and despair every day. My hope was entirely of the moment, tethered to surgery, drugs, and the long odds of a treatment and cure. After he died, I questioned whether I could ever trust in anyone or anything enough to experience real hope ever again, "And those who know your name put their trust in you, for you, O Lord, have not forsaken those who seek you" (Psalm 9:10).

After months of soul-searching, I knew that I must attempt to make a whole life for myself, whatever that might be. I knew that I could not live a diminished half-life, somehow "less than" because of the death of my husband. When one we love dies, there are gaping holes in our life that simply cannot be backfilled or paved over. We must navigate around the empty spaces to reach the solid ground on which to rebuild our lives.

I thought that if I could somehow reassemble the one million pieces of my shattered heart, my life would be whole again. I gathered the fragments into a pile but soon realized that I must first do some serious sorting. Tender reminders of a great earthly love were tucked into a special corner, so that I might revisit our shared joy at any time. Pieces with particularly jagged edges—slivers of failed relationships within a fractured family—were disposed of with regret, genuine sorrow, and some personal accountability. Other small fragments, the nuts and bolts of daily life that had no particular emotional investment, were simply put in the pile with other things from the past without too much thought or ceremony. By trial and sometimes painful error, I soon learned that working this very personal jigsaw puzzle was indeed an impossible task, nothing more or less than a folly of my grief. I could never put my life back together in exactly the same way that it once was. The pieces simply did not fit.

I shop from time to time at Whole Foods Market. When the first store opened in my area, I was curious about what it was selling. What exactly were *whole* foods? I wondered about the alternatives—half foods, incomplete foods, inferior foods? The store concept is to offer consumers organic, so-called natural foods. My experience, however, is that some organic foods and fruit that is picked prematurely have the same empty taste as food that is produced or farmed less sustainably. When fats and nutrients are removed from manufactured food, especially those labeled *natural*, the effect is usually the same—we eat more, in search of non-existent flavor. While this approach to grocery marketing has a certain modern street-level appeal, for most, wholeness is usually more subjective than absolute.

Over time, my growing desire for a whole life caused me to shift my spiritual focus away from self-help toward a more absolute trust in God, "I will give them a heart to know that I am the LORD; and they shall be my people and I will be their God, for they shall return to me with their whole heart" (Jeremiah 24:7). I knew that only faith could inspire me to hope again in life, "May the God of hope fill you with all joy and peace as you trust in him, so that you may overflow with hope by the power of the Holy Spirit" (Romans 15:13 NIV).

Wholeness, then, is evolutionary. It is a work in progress, so to speak. As our lives continually evolve, different pieces, new pieces acquired either by default or by design slowly mesh until they fit snugly together to create a whole life, our life, "...hold on to sound judgment and discretion . . . They will be life for your whole being, and an ornament for your neck" (Proverbs 3:21-22 CEB). Wholeness enables us to compartmentalize the past and live in the present. Wholeness allows us to claim our future, whatever it may be. Wholeness inspires hope, "there is hope for your future, says the LORD" (Jeremiah 31:17).

Wholeness is a byproduct of faith without boundaries. Wholeness is life without reservation. Wholeness is grounded not in greater self-sufficiency, but in deeper dependence on the presence of God, "I will give thanks to the LORD with my whole heart; I will tell of all your wonderful deeds" (Psalm 9:1).

OAKS OF
RIGHTEOUSNESS

They will be called oaks of righteousness,
the planting of the LORD, to display his glory.

—Isaiah 61:3

What might it mean to live as oaks of righteousness as the outcome of our experience of grief? Oaks are broadleaf trees that grow slowly to a massive height of approximately one hundred feet with a spread of fifty to eighty feet. They are a mighty and ancient botanical species that can live up to six hundred years.

So it towered high
above all the trees of the forest;
its boughs grew large
and its branches long,

—Ezekiel 31:5 RSV

The oak tree is a symbol of strength and endurance long identified with the gods and kings of the earliest tribes in Europe. Oaks were considered sacred by the Celts, a pre-Christian religious group from Gaul, Ireland, and Britain that flourished during the Iron Age. Celtic priests are known as *druids*, "those who know the oak." During the Classical Period in ancient Greece and through several periods of the

Roman Empire, wearing oak leaves signified royal status. To-day, bronze and silver oak leaf clusters are used to denote special merit and honor on some decorations and awards in the United States Armed Forces.

The oak is the national tree of Germany, the United Kingdom, and the United States. Because the oak tree symbolizes hospitality and safety, in some cultures, tradition holds that the best place to bury a child is close to an oak tree.

The acorn, the fruit of the oak tree, has come to symbolize the unlimited potential of a person to grow and endure. According to Scottish author Thomas Carlyle, "When the oak-tree is felled, the whole forest echoes with it; but a hundred acorns are planted silently by some unnoticed breeze."[10] When one we love dies, it feels as though the mighty oak of our life has been unceremoniously cut down. What seemed strong, durable, and invincible has been turned into little more than firewood by the death of one we love.

When we grieve, we are active participants in the cycle of life, death, and new life. Though we have been felled by one of the most painful experiences in all of life, we do not die. Rather, the tender acorns of our heart, our mind, our soul, and our spirit are silently planted to display the glory and presence of God, "The voice of the LORD causes the oaks to whirl, and strips the forest bare; and in his temple all say, "Glory!" (Psalm 29:9).

I will not die an unlived life
I will not live in fear
of falling or catching fire.
I choose to allow my living to open me,
to make me less afraid,
more accessible;
to loosen my heart

> until it becomes a wing,
> a torch, a promise.
> I choose to risk my significance,
> to live so that which came to me as seed
> goes to the next as blossom,
> and that which came to me as blossom,
> goes on as fruit.[11]

Over time, we grow in stature and strength until we become oaks of righteousness, "They will be called oaks of righteousness, the planting of the LORD, to display his glory" (Isaiah 61:3). Though the imagery suggested by the oak tree seems straightforward, reconciling righteousness and glory is sometimes more challenging. Yet it is through a heart of imperfect righteousness that we best glorify God, "Many are the afflictions of the righteous, but the LORD rescues them from them all" (Psalm 34:19).

Righteousness is about being in right relationship with God, "the righteous live by their faith" (Habakkuk 2:4). In grief, sometimes we wage war within our soul every day in tenacious pursuit of right relationship. We fight with ourselves and with God until one day we no longer name God as foe.

> Agree with God, and be at peace;
> in this way good will come to you.
> Receive instruction from his mouth,
> and lay up his words in your heart.
> If you return to the Almighty, you will be restored.

—Job 22:21-23

When we surrender our will to God and begin to grow as "the planting of the LORD," we claim the righteousness and peace that display the glory of God, "Blessed are those who hunger and thirst for righteousness, for they will be filled" (Matthew 5:6).

Righteousness is not about being right. Rather, it is about having a right purpose of soul. Spiritual righteousness begins with authentic goodness, a pure heart, and unmixed motives. A righteous spirit glorifies God, "He loves righteousness and justice; the earth is full of the steadfast love of the LORD" (Psalm 33:5).

We flourish and bear fruit to display the glory and presence of God, "And the trees of the field shall yield their fruit, and the earth shall yield its increase, and they shall be secure in their land. And they shall know that I am the LORD" (Ezekiel 34:27 ESV). As we grow in righteousness, we strain toward the light that filters through the dense greenery of our grief toward the warmth of God's love and faithful presence that transforms us into oaks of righteousness, "So they will be called oaks of righteousness, the planting of the LORD, that He may be glorified" (Isaiah 61:1-3 NASB).

GREEN LEAVES

Though the chill of winter sometimes lingers, the visual delights of spring renew our weather-weary spirit when trees all around us burst forth with the promise of new life. We trust the cycle of nature, even with its seasonal storms, floods, and other disruptive events. When we grieve, our trust in the order and predictability of life is shaken. The rhythm of our daily existence is suddenly unrooted, unalterably uprooted by the death of one we love.

Whether we realize it or not, when one we love dies we constantly assess the horizon of our trust. Who can we trust with the pain of our heart? How can we trust in life when death seems so random and unfair? We question the source and substance of our trust. If the root system of our life is nourished only by secular, superficial values, grief may direct our heart to search for spiritual values that are lasting, eternal, and truly trustworthy.

> Trust in the LORD with all your heart,
> and do not rely on your own insight.
> In all your ways acknowledge him,
> and he will make straight your paths.
>
> —Proverbs 3:5-6

Blessed is the man who trusts in the LORD,
whose trust in the LORD.
He is like a tree planted by water,
that sends out its roots by the stream,
and does not fear when heat comes,
for its leaves remain green,
and is not anxious in the year of drought,
for it does not cease to bear fruit.
—Jeremiah 17:7-8 RSV

In this passage, we are compared to a tree planted by water. I cherish a photo of my husband standing on the banks of a stream bordered by feathery green willow trees rustling softly in the breeze of an early summer day. It is a memory of a place "beside still waters" (Psalm 23:2 RSV) which always reminds me of our true spiritual roots.

When our life is firmly rooted in faith, we can withstand any loss.

They will come with weeping,
they will pray as I bring them back,
I will lead them beside streams of water
on a level path where they will not stumble.
—Jeremiah 31:9 NIV

Like a tree planted by water, our roots grow deep because we are planted close to the source of spiritual nourishment, "for its roots went down to abundant water" (Ezekiel 31:7). In trust our roots are alive and strong—we thrive in the presence of God, "the righteous will flourish like green leaves" (Proverbs 11:28).

For most, fear is a very real part of grief—fear before death, fear when our loved one dies, fear when we find ourselves alone. Though fear can choke the root system of our faith, our leaves remain green when we are firmly planted by the stream of living water that runs deeper than our grief.

> See, I am doing a new thing!
> Now it springs up; do you not perceive it?
> I am making a way in the wilderness
> and streams in the wasteland.

—Isaiah 43:19 NIV

With death comes an unexpected time of emotional and spiritual drought. Anxiety is fear magnified by the uncertainties of life without our loved one. Because we trust in God, the leaves of our life remain green.

> He is like a tree
> planted by streams of water,
> that yields its fruit in its season,
> and its leaf does not wither.
> In all that he does, he prospers.

—Psalm 1:3 RSV

We continue to bear fruit because our soul is forever rooted in the presence of God, "Those who abide in me and I in them bear much fruit, because apart from me you can do nothing" (John 15:5).

> The righteous flourish like the palm tree,
> and grow like a cedar in Lebanon.
> They are planted in the house of the LORD;
> they flourish in the courts of our God.
> In old age they still produce fruit;
> they are always green and full of sap,
> showing that the LORD is upright;
> he is my rock, and there is no
> unrighteousness in him.

—Psalm 92:12-15

THE HARVEST
OF GRIEF

I took a trip to a remote area of Wisconsin one year in mid-October. Because I had never been there before and had absolutely no idea where I was going, I researched, planned, and made the necessary arrangements to get there, wherever *there* was. I arrived on a rainy Sunday afternoon, picked up a rental car, and drove about a hundred miles almost due north.

After about an hour, I exited the interstate highway and drove "the road less traveled" through acres and acres of beautiful, expansive farmland with well-kept houses, towering silos, and large, pristine barns. For the most part, they were dairy farms dedicated to raising livestock and growing the crops that produce foodstuffs for both domestic use and export.

The fields were bare, the harvest was in. There is never a day of rest for those who depend on the earth and its cultivation for a living—the chores and cycle of farming are endless. There is always the next season and the next crop. Will there be enough rain? Are there sufficient nutrients in the soil to ensure the next harvest? Will the herd survive?

The work of grief is a little like farming. It is a challenging daily encounter with uncertainty and the possibility of setbacks and failure. The death of one we love destroys much of that which has been carefully planted and tended in what is now the fallow field of our life. We cannot envision any future harvest beyond our momentary grief. Yet we learn some of the most important fundamental lessons of personal cultivation from the experience of grief, "give, and it will be given to you. A good measure, pressed down, shaken together, running over, will be put into your lap; for the measure you give will be the measure you get back" (Luke 6:38).

Grief is farming our life—if we do not plant seeds, we cannot grow. We must farm the acreage of our soul and wait for the harvest, "Remember this: Whoever sows sparingly will also reap sparingly, and whoever sows generously will also reap generously. . . Now he who supplies seed to the sower and bread for food will also supply and increase your store of seed and will enlarge the harvest of your righteousness" (2 Corinthians 9:6,10 NIV).

As we furrow the expanse of our grief, we extract stones of guilt and regret that threaten to damage our plowshare, "But as for what was sown on good soil, this is the one who hears the word and understands it, who indeed bears fruit" (Matthew 13:23). Some stones may seem more like boulders. It takes time and extraordinary spiritual energy to pry unwieldy rocks from the soil of our mind and spirit. If we are to survive and grow forward, we cannot be defeated by weighty obstacles we may discover in the nutrient-starved ground of our soul, "So let us not grow weary in doing what is right, for we will reap at harvest time, if we do not give up" (Galatians 6:9).

Best practices in farming confirm that plowing in close rows is the most productive use of land. Close rows need less irrigation, allow fewer weeds to grow, and ultimately yield a larger crop. When we cultivate our soul and spirit, new life takes root and grows. As we carefully plow fresh new rows, we prepare our heart for the rest of our life, "My Father is glorified by this, that you bear much fruit" (John 15:8). If we plant seeds of fear, anger, and resentment, our harvest will be suspicion, mistrust, and bitterness. If we seed our heart with forbearance, patience, and love, in due season we reap a bountiful harvest of joy through the presence of God.

> May those who sow in tears
> reap with shouts of joy.
> Those who go out weeping,
> bearing the seed for sowing,
> shall come home with shouts of joy,
> carrying their sheaves.

—Psalm 126:5-6

FLYING OUT
IN FAITH

When I was a little girl, my beloved father came home from work around 5:30 p.m. His clockwork dependability endowed my young life with a sense of stability in an otherwise chaotic home environment.

I waited for my father to come home every day, listening for his car to pull into the driveway. As soon he emerged from the garage, I greeted him breathlessly with the question, "Daddy, can I fly to you?" With the exuberant joy of a child, I jumped spread-eagle into space with never a thought about whether I might crash to the pavement, oblivious to everything except the absolute exhilaration of being airborne, if only for a second. I knew without doubt that my father would drop his important-looking briefcase and extend his strong, waiting arms to catch me. The moment was one of joy and celebration as father and child affirmed their mutual trust in a single leap of faith.

And then one day I grew up. I was too big and too heavy for him to catch. In a word, I was too old to fly. Though this small ritual of unspoken love came to a natural end, by example my father taught me that God is dependable and completely reliable. In every small and large expression of his steadfast, unconditional love, my father modeled the very nature of God. I think now of how the simple act of flying out in faith expresses so well our absolute trust in the presence of God in our lives.

There are many small circus troupes that travel from town to town across Europe. In Freiburg, Germany Henri Nouwen had an unexpected experience of flying out in faith when he met and befriended The Flying Rodleighs one year when the Simoneit-Barum circus came to town. He shared this story:

> One day, I was sitting with Rodleigh, the leader of the troupe, in his caravan, talking about flying. He said, "As a flyer, I must have complete trust in my catcher. The public might think that I am the great star of the trapeze, but the real star is Joe, my catcher. He has to be there for me with split-second precision and grab me out of the air as I come to him in the long jump." "How does it work?" I asked. "The secret," Rodleigh said, "is that the flyer does nothing and the catcher does everything. When I fly to Joe, I have simply to stretch out my arms and hands and wait for him to catch me and pull me safely over the apron behind the catchbar."
>
> "You do nothing!" I said, surprised. "Nothing," Rodleigh repeated. "The worst thing the flyer can do is to try to catch the catcher. I am not supposed to catch Joe. It's Joe's task to catch me. If I grabbed Joe's wrists, I might break them, or he might break mine, and that would be the end for both of us. A flyer must fly, and a catcher must catch, and the flyer must trust, with outstretched arms, that his catcher will be there for him."

When Rodleigh said this with so much conviction, the words of Jesus flashed through my mind: "Father into your hands I commend my Spirit." Dying is trusting in the catcher. To care for the dying is to say, "Don't be afraid. Remember that you are the beloved child of God. He will be there when you make your long jump. Don't try to grab him; he will grab you. Just stretch out your arms and hands and trust, trust, trust."[12]

As he aged, my father began to show signs of physical and mental deterioration. It was my turn to be the catcher. He relied on my strong arms to hold him and carry him through to the end of his life. He honored me with his unreserved trust, graciously offered in full confidence that I would be there for him until the end, just as he had been there for me when I needed him to be the catcher.

Surely it is one of God's greatest delights when we fly into God's waiting, outstretched arms with abandon and absolute faith, especially when we grieve. Though all else is changed when one we love dies, in the assurance of our faith we know that God is utterly dependable. We know that God will never let us fall. We know that God will never let us go. We know that God is present to us always, "For you have delivered my soul from death, my eyes from tears, my feet from stumbling" (Psalm 116:8).

A GARLAND

The spirit of the Lord God is upon me...
he has sent me to bring good news to the oppressed,
to bind up the brokenhearted...
to comfort all who mourn...to give them a garland
instead of ashes.

—Isaiah 61:1, 3

There is a certain implied beauty in the word *garland*, which rolls off the tongue like a delicious liquid. In ancient Greece and other periods in which history and mythology were frequently intertwined, garlands were used as a symbol of victory, power, honor, achievement, and even love. Garlands were usually made of laurel leaves, woven into a wreath or crown or a continuous length that was worn around the neck, "for they are a graceful garland for your head and pendants for your neck" (Proverbs 1:9 ESV).

Beginning in 776 BCE, those who were victorious in athletic competitions were crowned with wreaths of laurel leaves, much like the Olympic medals awarded today. The laurel leaf is from the Mediterranean bay laurel tree. Anyone who cooks probably has dried bay leaves on a spice rack tucked in with other herbs and spices. When bay leaves are tossed into a pot of soup or sauce, generally we are more interested in their subtle flavor than in their historic significance.

I was once in a play set in Crete around 1200 BCE. After the performance, an admirer presented me with a laurel wreath crafted from bay leaves carefully glued together to form a flat semi-circular crown as a token of congratulations. Though at the time I did not fully understand its historic or symbolic significance, I was more touched by the small crown of laurel leaves than if I had received a dozen red roses, "She will place on your head a fair garland; she will bestow on you a beautiful crown" (Proverbs 4:9).

Throughout history, laurel wreaths have been given to honor achievement in literature, government, education, and the arts. In education, the terms *baccalaureate* and *bachelor* are derived from the word *baccalareus*, or laurel berry. According to Roman tradition, great scholars or poets, known as *laureates*, were recognized with an award of laurel wreaths. Even today, those who are honored for their outstanding creative or intellectual achievement are designated as laureates—poet laureates, Nobel laureates.

The laurel also became a symbol of power for military leaders, kings, and emperors. As the self-proclaimed supreme leader of the Roman Republic, Caesar ensured that during his reign, he alone wore a laurel wreath crown crafted from gold and precious stones. Following the decline of the Greek and Roman empires, the use of the laurel wreath as an emblem of power declined and did not re-emerge until the Middle Ages. In 1804 Napoleon claimed supreme power when he declared himself emperor of France, symbolized by a gold crown of laurel leaves.

A *lei* is a garland originally worn by ancient Polynesians that is still used by native Hawaiians to signify rank or royalty. Leis symbolize celebration, honor, friendship, and love. Typically they are given to greet someone who arrives or departs the islands. The colors and intoxicating scent of the flowers used to create leis easily rival the traditional laurel leaf garland in both beauty and splendor.

We are assured in Scripture that the ashes of our grief will be rewarded with a garland of praise. Thanks be to God for the garland that celebrates our victory over death through the presence of God, "On that day, the LORD of heavenly forces will be a splendid garland and a beautiful wreath for the people who survive" (Isaiah 28:5 CEB).

OUR SAINTS IN
CIRCULATION

B ecause our experience of grief is both intimate and personal, we may choose to memorialize our loved ones
more privately than publicly. When we invite others into
the sacred space of our grief, we share our story of love and
loss with those in need of community and spiritual encouragement. As we open our heart to close family members,
acquaintances, or even relative strangers, we put our saints
in circulation.

During the seventeenth-century reign of Oliver
Cromwell in Great Britain, the government ran low on silver
for coins. Cromwell sent his men out to local cathedrals to
see if they could find any precious metals. They reported,
"The only silver we could find is in the statues of the saints
standing in the corners." Cromwell replied, "Good! We'll
melt them down and put them into circulation!"[13] Those
we love in life and remember in death are the saints of our
lives. Their eternal qualities are our enduring lasting legacy,
the coin of our realm. We put our saints in circulation when
their spiritual gifts live on both in us, and through us long
after they die.

Some describe those whose lives are well-lived as *durable*
saints. When I consider those who have enriched my life
emotionally and spiritually, I remember my beloved hus-

band with heartfelt gratitude for his profound influence on my life and on the lives of countless others through his inspired ministry. I remember my father, who embodied the love of God the Father. The sustained presence of durable saints in our lives assures our heart of all that is eternal.

Rev. Paul Escamilla offers this reflection on durable saints, "Among the varied ways faithfulness has become the fabric of their lives, one quality has been identifiable again and again . . . a certain adequacy of means that issues forth in abundance for others."

He continues, "At their passing, these durable saints have signed the air not so much with fanfare as grace. The ledgers of their lives are long in matters of generosity, self-giving, and trust; more measured in the realm of acquisition and possessions; and slimmest of all in regard to recognition and self-promotion. In other words, over a lifetime they seem . . . to have needed little and offered much."[14]

We give thanks to God for the saints in our lives who have blessed us with their love, authentic goodness, kindness, compassion, and sterling faith. We learn from our durable saints that the most valuable inheritance we leave to those we love is the essence of ourselves. The endowments of our spirit will always be present to those we love who will grieve for a while in this certainty, "He will wipe every tear from their eyes. There will be no more death or mourning or crying or pain, for the old order of things has passed away" (Revelation 21:4 NIV).

Through the eternal, everlasting presence of God, both in life and in death we are saints in circulation, "We do not live to ourselves, and we do not die to ourselves. If we live, we live to the Lord, and if we die, we die to the Lord; so then, whether we live or die, we are the Lord's" (Romans 14:7-8).

FRAGILE JOY

As we emerge from the experience of grief and the structure of life begins to take on new shape, we may feel tentative about rejoining the world, "But whoever is joined with all the living has hope" (Ecclesiastes 9:4). When we are beyond the worst of our grief, outwardly we may seem relatively strong and unchanged, yet our inner dialogue continues to churn around our willingness to hope, our readiness to risk, and our capacity for joy.

When the death of one we love has shaken the very foundation of our lives, we question whether our life will ever again be more about joy and less about death and grief. At some point, most who grieve acknowledge at least intellectually, if not emotionally that the one we love who is no longer here would want us to live a rich, joy-filled life, whatever that might mean to us. Our somewhat unrealistic expectation is that we should be able to experience and fully embrace joy today, right now, however fragile joy may feel.

We do not simply put aside the emotions of grief once and for all time. As we near the end of active grief, we discover that joy requires a certain single-minded discipline of spirit. We relearn joy slowly, almost imperceptibly, as we abandon past resentments, unfulfilled hopes, and put away our dreams of all that might have been, "do not be grieved, for the joy of the LORD is your strength" (Nehemiah 8:10).

Some may obstinately resist joy. The apostle Thomas was both a pragmatist and a skeptic who had no use for secondhand joy. He needed proof before he could enter into joy.

> But Thomas (who was called the Twin), one of the twelve, was not with them when Jesus came. So the other disciples told him, "We have seen the Lord." But he said to them, "Unless I see the mark of the nails in his hands, and put my finger in the mark of the nails and my hand in his side, I will not believe."
> A week later his disciples were again in the house, and Thomas was with them. Although the doors were shut, Jesus came and stood among them and said, "Peace be with you." Then he said to Thomas, "Put your finger here and see my hands. Reach out your hand and put it in my side. Do not doubt but believe." Thomas answered him, "My Lord and my God!" Jesus said to him, "Have you believed because you have seen me? Blessed are those who have not seen and yet have come to believe."

—John 20:24-29

Only incontrovertible evidence could persuade the original "Doubting Thomas" to trust a sacred moment of recognition and joy. We grow in faith when we yield our heart to whispers of love and memory that stir our heart to fragile joy.

When we experience the death of one we love, for a while we may feel apprehensive about trusting in life again. Some develop the habit of "waiting for the other shoe to drop," certain that life will be an ongoing series of events that verge on disaster. Each small calamity reinforces our momentary conviction that life will never be good again, that joy is an experience of the past. The first faint quivers of fragile joy require an emotional commitment. Do we reenter the mainstream and trust in life again? How do we reconcile the pain and sorrow of death with the possibility of a lifetime of joy?

When a baby is born, we experience a kind of fragile joy, a joy that is charged with hope and expectation. Though we know with certainty that life will not be perfect beyond the divine moment of birth, we do not reject the perfection of a baby because of possible adversity at some distant time in life. With a heart overflowing with love and gratitude, we enter wholeheartedly into the moment of fragile joy that teeters between celebration of new life and the unknown future.

On a blustery fall day, I felt a kind of fragile joy as I watched the last leaves of autumn chatter across the road in a sudden gust of wind. Though there was no real rationale for my surge of feeling, I knew that it was joy—joy to be alive, joy to be able to see the beauty of nature in all its fading glory, joy simply to be in the world. There are many wisps of fragile joy all around us if we will open our hearts and capture them. We celebrate the enduring power of joy when warm memories of a shared song, a place, or a holiday tradition evoke fragile joy rather than tears. When we grieve, we may need to redevelop the muscle memory of our heart before we can once again fully enter into the experience of joy, "Light dawns for the righteous, and joy for the upright in heart" (Psalm 97:11).

Joy looks different on the other side of grief. It is richer and deeper; it saturates our soul with hope, "I will turn their mourning into joy, I will comfort them, and give them gladness for sorrow" (Jeremiah 31:13). The presence of God is at the epicenter of every breath and loud shout of joy, "Be glad in the Lord and rejoice, O righteous, and shout for joy, all you upright in heart" (Psalm 32:11).

PART IV

EMMANUEL: GOD PRESENT TO US

FORGIVING

When we grieve at the holidays, deep within our being we feel the contradiction between sorrow and seasonal joy, sadness and good cheer, loneliness and festive gatherings. As our spirit spins, the season seems like an emotional blur.

A *kaleidoscope* is an optical instrument that operates on the principle of reflection. Typically, there are two or more mirrors angled inside the cylinder. At one end there is a cell with loose, colored pieces of glass or other transparent materials. When we put our eye against the small opening, direct the other end toward the light, then rotate the cell, we see an ever-changing variety of symmetrical patterns in an almost limitless spectrum of colors. There is nothing predictable about a kaleidoscope. The images we see are random, much like our feelings of grief at the holidays. If we look intently, we see the rich, kaleidoscopic reflection of life beyond our grief through the light of the presence of God.

When we grieve, the pain of loss is easily exacerbated by holidays. Whether we prepare to host and entertain, or we are an invited guest at a festive celebration, instinctively we brace for occasions that have the potential to evoke high emotions. However we plan, grief will be an inevitable part of our gathering with friends and family. Even if those who come together are grieving the same loved one, no one's experience of grief is ever exactly the same. If the family has lost its matriarch or patriarch, each child grieves differently. No one's grief is the same as that of the surviving spouse—for better or for worse. If an entire family is grieving the loss of a beloved child, there may be many shared moments of heartbreak and remembrance. For every loss, there is a very personal grief.

When we are confronted with a stereotypical picture of what a family gathering should look like, as in many Norman Rockwell illustrations, we are easily convinced that the image portrayed is the ideal. However, what we experience in real life is that each family—biological, blended, or chosen—has its own unique dynamic. In many families, dysfunction, addiction, in-laws, out-laws, and step-*everyones* make the holidays at best a challenge, with or without the extra dimension of grief.

Our feelings are especially vulnerable at the holidays. Emotions may bubble to the surface and erupt at unexpected times, in unexpected ways. During the season, likely we will encounter someone who has neglected us during the worst of our grief, someone who was a conspicuous "no-show" at the time of our loss, a relative who could not "handle it", or someone who said a thoughtless word that we associate with them and the death of the one we love. Or we may be thrown together with others who have chosen simply to ignore our pain and act like nothing happened. Generally they are clueless because they have not yet experienced the death of one they love. In these moments, forgiveness is not optional. Rather, forgiveness is essential for surviving the holiday season.

In the moment, our pain and sorrow may not allow us to meet these "others" where they are with the gift of unconditional forgiveness. Yet we can get close to forgiveness if we simply let go of the resentments, hurts, and anger we have carefully put aside or stuffed down somewhere deep inside us. Though our heart may well have a long memory and stubbornly hold on to perceived wrongs, forgiveness requires that we release those who have been thoughtless or inconsiderate from being hostage to our grief. When we forgive, we begin to heal the wounds inflicted by the past and exchange our pain for present peace. In forgiveness, we always prevail, "'Do not judge, and you will not be judged; do not condemn, and you will not be condemned. Forgive, and you will be forgiven'" (Luke 6:37).

Forgiveness is an act of human grace that calms our soul, especially when we grieve at the holidays. Forgiveness is the better part of love that honors the memory of the one we hold dear and moves us forward in life toward reconciliation and joy, "be kind to one another, tenderhearted, forgiving one another, as God in Christ has forgiven you" (Ephesians 4:32). In forgiveness, we stand in the full light of the presence of God, Emmanuel, God with us.

FORGETTING

Even if we have done the work of forgiveness, when the dying coals of unpleasant memories and negative experiences are kindled to life by some reminder from the past, it is not always our first response to douse the flames, especially at the holidays. Sometimes our first impulse is to cozy up to the fire, make some s'mores, and warm our indignation by the roaring fire of our hurt and self-justification.

When we grieve at the holidays, the fires of our memory easily find the oxygen and fuel to live and grow. If we cannot seem to forget what has happened, we may find ourselves engulfed in a raging blaze of conversation with ourself, which begins with the misdeeds of others and ends with our need for emotional vindication.

Though we may master forgiveness, forgetting is sometimes much easier said than done. When our heart is broken by the death of one we love, we remember the state of our mind and heart at a time in life when we were most fragile and vulnerable. For some, that time may be now. Though our instinct may be to duck and run when we see those who have hurt us or added to our pain, we waste valuable emotional energy when we tenaciously remember the slights of others. We are the ones who suffer if we hang on to inept, hurtful words or harbor resentment toward those who have tried to comfort us but have said exactly the wrong thing.

More often than not, the *doer* is oblivious or has completely forgotten. Scraping back through the unpleasantness of what is over and done is an easy habit to fuel. No matter how much emotional energy we expend to stir the ashes, the outcome will always be the same. We take an important step forward in rebuilding our lives when we learn to forget.

If we are exhausted by all the emotional "fire drills" and are ready—really ready—to let go and forget, mentally we must "stop, drop, and roll." By doing something proactive, we direct our mind away from negative thoughts when they resurface from time to time, especially at the holidays.

Forgetting takes practice. Remembering can easily be fanned into flames and threaten our spiritual resolve to forget, "You will forget your misery; you will remember it as waters that have passed away" (Job 11:16). Forgetting is like having a handy fire extinguisher strapped to our toolbelt of life—it is an essential piece of survival equipment, a lasting takeaway from our singular experience of love and loss and grief. The best response of our spirit is not only to forgive, but also to forget. Forgetting unkind words and hurtful incidents is the best holiday gift we can give to others and to ourselves.

Whatever the nature of our relationship with the one now lost to us in death—intense love, uneasy tolerance, or somewhere in between—we honor the sacred trust of a shared life when we forget the forgettable and hold fast to our most cherished, unforgettable memories, "Bless the LORD, O my soul, and do not forget all his benefits" (Psalm 103:2). In the life-giving joy of release, we experience the presence of God, now, always, and at this season of holy remembrance, "'they shall name him Emmanuel,' which means, 'God is with us'" (Matthew 1:23).

THE GLOW

A t a museum gift shop one year, I selected some Christ-mas cards and asked a sales associate to explain the "buy one box and get half off the second box" promotional offer. As we discussed the math, I felt the woman sizing me up, trying to decide whether I was friend or foe because I dared to challenge the logic of the *deal*. In fact, I was neither. I was just one more Christmas shopper trying to buy something on sale.

When we turned the corner in our conversation and got to a meeting of the minds about the price, we exchanged a small smile of mutual relief and finished the transaction. Before I turned to leave, she said rather shyly, "Your skin has such a nice glow."

I was surprised by the compliment. Perhaps she hoped I would share some skincare secret with her, or maybe she made the remark because I had used too much of a good thing. As it happened, that very day I had purchased a new product that practically guaranteed a radiant glow. I was deeply touched by her personal outreach and quietly said "thank you" as I left. At the time, it seemed the better part of grace simply to acknowledge her kindness and be on my way.

As I returned to the city streets, I thought about the encounter and where our glow really comes from, especially when we grieve. In the waning hours of the day, I watched people walking along, staring at smartphones that cast an eerie green glow on their faces. I saw others with the reflected glow of lights and tinsel shining in their cold-kissed faces.

Christmas is about the light of the world that reaches into our heart to illuminate our darkness. When we grieve, we seek the light that inspires our glow, "in your light we see light" (Psalm 36:9). Our glow shines brightly when hope for the future overcomes our sadness. Our glow is brighter still when we move toward acceptance and its life-renewing peace. The glow of Christmas shines in small, private moments when our heart is strangely warmed by the presence of God. The mystery of God's divine love enlightens our soul with the assurance that there is life beyond the death of one we love.

In my brief retail experience with a lovely woman in the secular world of pre-Christmas shopping, I discovered yet again that our glow within comes only from the light of God. Christmas comes when we receive an unexpected blessing. Christmas comes when we are a blessing to others. The presence of God is the radiant glow that guides us safely through the season of celebration and lights our way through grief at Christmas, "'I am the light of the world. Whoever follows me will never walk in darkness but will have the light of life'" (John 8:12).

THE ORPHANS

The Dallas Arboretum is an urban oasis of natural and man-made beauty on the banks of a lake not far from downtown. This lovely place has been a refuge, especially since the death of my beloved husband. Before he died, we enjoyed going there together; after he died it became my grieving place "beside still waters."

On a crisp December afternoon three days before Christmas one year, I went to the Arboretum to find a peaceful moment of "all is calm, all is bright." I left refreshed by the exquisite beauty of the clear, cool day and the feeling of being far removed from the noise of the city and the season.

As I walked toward the exit, my eyes fell on a display outside the gift shop. In what appeared to be a last-ditch effort to sell the remainder of the Christmas merchandise, there was a stand of long, decorated sticks intended as ornaments for a garden or yard.

They were pretty well picked over—the ones that were left at the end of the season seemed somehow sad and pitiful. An imperfect Santa leaned against a sign that proclaimed "blessings." Several sagging soldiers were mixed in with a few lopsided angels. These were the decorations no one wanted. They were the unwanted, inanimate *orphans* of yet another season of intense commercialism. Their abandonment drew me in.

On the way home, I stopped by a megastore for a container to hold one last batch of Christmas cookies. Though the store was already winding down for Christmas, on the aisle with the last of the stocking candy and desperation gifts for last-minute shoppers, I saw other orphans—plastic knick-knacks in faded seasonal colors, slightly dented tins, and the last tired ribbons and wrapping paper.

Since that day, I have thought about orphans and the loneliness of grief, especially at Christmas. There is surely nothing more heartbreaking than a child of any age without the love, affection, and protection of a caring adult, whether a natural parent, an adoptive parent, a foster parent, or someone who needs the two-way blessing that only a child can offer, "Give justice to the weak and the orphan; maintain the right of the lowly and the destitute. Rescue the weak and the needy" (Psalm 82:3-4). However orphaned we may feel as we grieve at Christmas, God is present—we are never alone, "For all who are led by the Spirit of God are children of God" (Romans 8:14).

There are spiritual orphans all around us who need an outstretched hand of love, welcome, and inclusion, especially at Christmas. Perhaps we are orphaned by social isolation because we have little connection to friends or a place of community. Perhaps we are orphaned by circumstance if we are quarantined or restricted in our physical contact with others by an infectious disease or pandemic. Perhaps we are orphaned by a rupture in our family that seems irreparable, at least for the time being. I sat next to a woman at church one year on Christmas Eve who was estranged from her husband and children. Tearfully, she poured out her heart because she felt so alone and abandoned. She was an orphan in need of hope, comfort, and love, especially on that holy night.

God is with us when we feel forgotten, lost, and lonely, especially at Christmas. Though we are separated by death from the one we love, there are no spiritual orphans in the presence of God, "'I will never leave you or forsake you'" (Hebrews 13:5).

THE ANGEL WORE
SNEAKERS

…not just any old work shoes, but hot pink sneakers with shiny silver racing stripes. This particular angel had bright yellow curly hair, the perfect complement to her sunny disposition. She was the flower lady responsible for seasonal arrangements in the large gothic dining room of an historic estate house. Her job was to arrange and care for the vibrant displays of fresh Christmas greenery and flowers which brightened that moody space with its soaring cathedral ceilings.

As I toured through the oversized rooms of the vast estate on Christmas Eve, I realized that my spirit was unwilling to settle for an entirely secular holiday celebration. My head and heart loudly insisted on a spiritual experience of Christmas far beyond mere candles and wreaths. I wanted nothing more than to hear the angels sing.

When I entered the dining room, the angel in sneakers smiled brightly and asked with a broad Southern accent, "How are you today, Hon?" She was the spirit of pure joy, the light amid the gloom, the sun that warmed my heart on that bleak midwinter day. Tears flooded my eyes, for at that very moment the massive pipe organ in the balcony began to play my favorite Christmas carol, "Angels We Have Heard on High." In that shining moment, the noise and tinsel of the world faded away. For a twinkling, my spirit stood in the sacred presence of God.

When we grieve, sometimes a word or gesture of comfort and grace from a stranger is more powerful than the hollow echo of empty platitudes, especially at the holidays. When someone meets us at the right place at the right time with a word or silent embrace, we are enfolded in the love and presence of God. Whether or not we believe in angels, grief heightens our awareness of those whom God uses to minister to us when we least expect it. This is the power of the presence of God, Emmanuel, God with us.

In truth, the bright pink sneakers were the last thing about this special angel that got my attention that day. It was her pure, gossamer spirit and tender kindness that stilled my soul and spoke God's love to me. And if this one angel could reach into my forlorn, needy heart on that dreary Christmas Eve, how much more is God present to us every minute of our lives, especially when we grieve? In her warm spirit, her caring outreach to others, her meticulous attention to the beauty of the flowers she so gracefully tended, I saw the presence of God. My soul took flight, my spirit soared, "And suddenly there was with the angel a multitude of the heavenly host praising God, and saying, Glory to God in the highest, and on earth peace, good will toward men" (Luke 2:13-14 KJV).

THE NOISE OF
CHRISTMAS

On a museum visit a few days before Christmas, an exhibit I especially wanted to see was on display in a remote corner of the top floor. Perhaps the idea behind this strategic location was to get visitors to hike through some of the less-frequented areas of the museum. Indeed, it was quite a feat to find the room on the map and trek down the long, winding corridors. When I got there, I was alone. It seemed I was the only person interested in blue and white porcelain on that particular December day.

It was blissfully silent, almost unnaturally quiet. As I stood there admiring the artistry of each individual piece, I became aware of a noise, an insistent tap-tap-tapping headed in my direction. My first thought was, "Who wears rude shoes to a museum?" My notion of a museum as a place of relative quiet was challenged by the loud approach of someone who had just as much right to be there as I did.

Shame and self-reproach washed through my soul as I saw a young, visually impaired man making his way down the hall, assisted by the steady arm of a companion and the sure sight of his long cane. When our paths crossed, he made a U-turn and kept walking. Though he perhaps sensed my presence, he was completely focused on moving ahead.

I sat down for a moment and considered the noise so necessary for his connection to life. I wondered, too, what a blind man could see in a museum. Perhaps he was there to gain the confidence necessary for a life of self-determination and independence. While I was there simply to look at man-made beauty, he was there to explore the world. Disturbed by my rush to judgment, I left deep in thought about the noise that constantly surrounds us and the spiritual blindness that sometimes convicts us.

A well-known quote is attributed to Helen Keller, who was both blind and deaf, "The only thing worse than being blind is having sight but no vision."[15] Gratefully, most of us will never know what it feels like to be blind and live in darkness or to be deaf and live in silence. Yet when we grieve the death of one we love, we may feel spiritually blind for a while. We grope our way through the darkness of grief because we cannot see the light of new life. In the presence of God, our heart is transformed from darkness into light. In Emmanuel, we behold a clear vision for the rest of our lives.

Though we would like it to be otherwise, we cannot will our grief to be over just because it is Christmas. As the sounds of Advent urge us yet again toward the manger, we may need to listen through the darkness of our grief and follow the noise of the season, "Let me hear joy and gladness" (Psalm 51:8). For perhaps the birth of Christ was not such a "silent night" after all. Jesus was born into the noise of earthly life—the clip-clop of a weary donkey, the insistent sounds of hungry manger animals, the sighs of a mother in labor. If we do not pay attention to the noise, we may miss the experience of Christmas, "And the shepherds returned, glorifying and praising God for all the things that they had heard and seen, as it was told unto them" (Luke 2:20 KJV).

With the heavenly music of an entire chorus of angels and the brilliant light of a radiant star, God proclaims that a savior is born to all the world. As we kneel in awe and wonder before Christ the Lord in the presence of God incarnate, may the carols of our soul be the most beautiful noise of all, "Make a joyful noise to the Lord, all the earth" (Psalm 100:1). In an exquisite moment of Christmas may we see, hear, and receive the love of Emmanuel, God with us.

TRANSACTIONAL
JOY

As I was returning to the airport on a rainy Sunday afternoon after speaking at a Christmas service of remembrance, I saw a drive-through restaurant and decided to get a cold drink before turning onto the highway for the fifty-mile drive. There was no car ahead of mine, so I placed my order and proceeded to the window.

The woman who greeted me was not a typical fast-food employee. She looked much older than she probably was. Perhaps she had done some hard living or been a victim of challenging circumstance in her life. Her mostly gray hair was tied back haphazardly and revealed a face with a story to tell, its chapters etched into the wrinkles and folds of her leathery skin.

Yet her charming, rather lopsided smile was radiant and drew me in. Her warm, engaging spirit suggested that with every transaction and personal interaction, there was the possibility of a new friend. Her manner and outreach far exceeded any standard customer greeting suggested by the company handbook. In that brief moment of enterprise—I gave her $1.81, she gave me a cold drink—there was an experience of transactional joy that touched me deeply. I left certain that for one shining instant I had been in the presence of an unlikely angel.

In John 16:20 (NIV) we read this intimation of joy, "Very truly I tell you, you will weep and mourn while the world rejoices. You will grieve, but your grief will turn to joy." The promise grows more exciting in verse 22, "Now is your time of grief, but I will see you again and you will rejoice, and no one will take away your joy." While both verses clearly acknowledge the reality of our grief, they overflow with hope and the promise of joy.

When we grieve at Christmas, there may be a vast disconnect between superficial merrymaking and the transactional joy of Christmas. We may be surrounded by friends, family, and those we call family, yet we may be unable or unwilling to enter into the organized good cheer of a seasonal gathering. We ask, "What's wrong with me?" because we are longing for the presence of our loved one. Transactional joy cannot be experienced in emotional isolation. There are always two parties to any transaction.

One of my small Christmas traditions is to donate to the Salvation Army Red Kettle drive. For many years, there was a red kettle right outside my local drugstore, complete with the seasonal high spirits and persistent bell ringing of a volunteer soliciting donations. With the advance of technology and increased concern about safety and security, in recent years the only place to donate has been at a local mall. Instead of a red kettle waiting to be stuffed with crumpled bills, there is a red tripod with only a forlorn, dangling chain. Instead of a volunteer, there is a sign on how to donate by text. Though an electronic transaction lacks the satisfaction and pure joy of a human interaction, for those in need it makes no difference whether blessings come from cyberspace or a red kettle.

Christmas comes when our hearts are touched by joy. Within every transaction of our soul and spirit there is Emmanuel, God with us, "But the angel said to them, 'Do not be afraid; for see—I am bringing you good news of great joy for all the people'" (Luke 2:10). Christmas comes when someone—a friend, a relative, or a complete stranger—reaches out to us in love. Christmas comes when we reach out to someone else in love—a friend, a relative, or a complete stranger—with no expectation other than the potential for joy—their joy and ours.

At the heart of transactional joy is the presence of God, the source of all true joy, "When they saw that the star had stopped, they were overwhelmed with joy. On entering the house, they saw the child with Mary his mother; and they knelt down and paid him homage. Then, opening their treasure chests, they offered him gifts of gold, frankincense, and myrrh" (Matthew 2:10-11).

REGIFTING

Giving something that we have received to someone else is known as *regifting*, a practice that has been around for a long time but that has become more openly acceptable in recent years. The urge to recycle our stuff is driven by a desire to rid ourselves of those things we do not want or need and will never use. We think that our castoffs might be used or enjoyed by someone else, so we pass them along as *gifts*.

According to one survey, more than half of all adults agree that regifting is not objectionable if it is done with consideration and respect. Etiquette experts generally agree on a few fundamental guidelines for regifting:

- Whatever the gift, someone has made the effort to give it. Before regifting, the giver should be sincerely thanked for his or her thoughtfulness.

- To qualify for regifting, the gift/merchandise must be in perfect condition, in its original packaging, with the instructions.

- The regifted item must be something the recipient really needs or would like to have.

- The gift is not something that is one-of-a-kind, handmade, or personalized.

– Never regift something to the original giver.

– Never regift something to someone who might know the original giver.

– Remember that an unwanted gift could be a welcome donation to a charitable organization.

When we grieve, those who offer consolation regift their own emotions. Each expression of comfort comes from the heart and life experience of another. Our empathy, compassion, and love grow as life is informed and enriched by each experience of death and grief,

"For who has known the mind of the Lord?
Or who has been his counselor?"
"Or who has given a gift to him,
to receive a gift in return?"
For from him and through him and to him are
all things.
To him be the glory forever. Amen.

—Romans 11:34-36

When we are blessed by the gift of comfort, we regift to others the comfort we ourselves have received from God, "Praise be to the God and Father of our Lord Jesus Christ, the Father of compassion and the God of all comfort, who comforts us in all our troubles, so that we can comfort those in any trouble with the comfort we ourselves receive from God" (2 Corinthians 1:3-4 NIV).

God created us to love, "you shall love the Lord your God with all your heart, and with all your soul, and with all your mind" (Mark 12:30). We regift God's love to us and our love for God as we love others. Yet from the limited sightline of our mortality, it is impossible to fully grasp the enormity of God's love, "I pray that you may have the power to comprehend, with all the saints, what is the breadth and length and height and depth, and to know the love of Christ that surpasses knowledge, so that you may be filled with all the fullness of God" (Ephesians 3:18-19).

Spiritual regifting is circular, "Every good gift, every perfect gift, comes from above" (James 1:17 CEB). As we offer our gifts of grief to others, we experience the exponential power of regifting to comfort and bless those who grieve. When we regift our personal gifts and graces to others, we find new life, "We have gifts that differ according to the grace given to us: prophecy, in proportion to faith; ministry, in ministering; the teacher, in teaching; the exhorter, in exhortation; the giver, in generosity; the leader, in diligence; the compassionate, in cheerfulness" (Romans 12:6-8).

In the presence of God, we receive the gifts of divine light and heavenly joy. In Emmanuel, God with us, we triumph over death and grief in the One who is the way, the truth, and the life, "For unto you is born this day in the city of David a Saviour, which is Christ the Lord" (Luke 2:11 KJV).

In the bleak mid-winter,
Frosty wind made moan,
Earth stood hard as iron,
Water like a stone;
Snow had fallen, snow on snow,
Snow on snow,
In the bleak midwinter,
Long ago.

Our God, Heaven cannot hold Him,
Nor earth sustain,
Heaven and earth shall flee away
When He comes to reign.
In the bleak mid-winter
A stable-place sufficed
The Lord God Almighty—
Jesus Christ.

Enough for Him, whom cherubim
Worship night and day,
A breastful of milk,
And a mangerful of hay;
Enough for Him, whom Angels
Fall down before,
The ox and ass and camel
Which adore.

Angels and archangels
May have gathered there,
Cherubim and seraphim
Thronged the air;
But only His mother
In her maiden bliss,
Worshipped the Beloved
With a kiss.

What can I give Him,
Poor as I am?—
If I were a Shepherd,
I would bring a lamb;
If I were a Wise Man,
I would do my part,—
Yet what I can I give Him,—
Give my heart.[16]

NOTES

1. The United Methodist Book of Worship, (Nashville, Tenn: United Methodist Publishing House, ©1992), Number 464, Ruth Duck.

2. Horatius Bonar, "The Love of God," *Hymns of Faith and Hope,* second series (New York: Robert Carter & Brothers, 1862), 52–54.

3. Minnie Louise Haskins, "God Knows", *Desert (1908).*

4. Julie Turkewitz, "'I Want This to Get Over': After Congressional Shooting, Complex Grief for a Gunman's Widow," New York Times (July 1, 2017), https://www.nytimes.com/2017/07/01/us/congressional-baseball-shooting-death-grief.html, accessed November 2, 2020.

5. Juan A. Lozano and Claire Galofaro, "Texas mourners endure grief that 'none of us can comprehend'," AP News (May 20, 2018), https://apnews.com/article/ee2b420523b-94825ba8366fe3ef8a1e8, accessed November 2, 2020.

6. Percy Bysshe Shelley, "To a Skylark," *The Oxford Book of English Verse: 1250–1900*, Arthur Thomas Quiller-Couch, ed. (Oxford: Clarendon, 1900), 705.

7. "The Burial of the Dead: Rite One," The Book of Common Prayer (Church Publishing, Inc., 2011), 485.

8. Richard Rohr, "Grieving as Sacred Space," Sojourners (January-February 2002), https://sojo.net/magazine/january-february-2002/grieving-sacred-space, accessed November 3, 2020.

9. Wayne Muller, *A Life of Being, Having, and Doing Enough* (New York, Three Rivers Press, 2010), 113.

10. Thomas Carlyle, "On History," *A Carlyle Reader*, G. B. Tennyson, ed. (London: Cambridge University Press, 1984), 58.

11. Dawna Markova, *I Will Not Die an Unlived Life; Reclaiming Passion and Purpose* (Berkeley, CA: Conari Press, 2000), 2. Used with permission - DawnaMarkova.com

12. *The Essential Henri Nouwen*, edited by Robert A. Jonas (Boston: Shambhala Publications, Inc., 2009), 131–32.

13. https://commonplacefacts.wordpress.com/2019/09/27/melting-and-circulating-the-saints/, accessed November 24, 2020.

14. Paul Escamilla, *Longing for Enough in a Culture of More* (Nashville, Abingdon Press, 2007), 4-5.

15. https://www.goodreads.com/quotes/6497288-the-only-thing-worse-than-being-blind-is-having-sight, accessed November 24, 2020.

16. Christina Rossetti, "A Christmas Carol," as published in Scribner's Monthly (January 1872).

About the Author

Julie Yarbrough has written extensively on grief, inspired by the death of her beloved husband. She is the author of the *Beyond the Broken Heart* grief group resources and other books that address the practical and spiritual challenges of grief. In writing about grief, her premise is that those who grieve seek answers found only when they understand their personal experience of grief.

Present Comfort is for those who have experienced personal loss and for those who are at a loss to understand the range of emotions specific to grief. The meditations in *Present Comfort* offer assurance, encouragement, and spiritual insight for those who grieve, and context for those who desire to share in the heart and language of grief. The hope is that *Present Comfort* will inspire a deeper faith that in each whisper of comfort, there is the presence of God.

Julie lives in Dallas, Texas and is President of Yarbrough Investments. She serves on the Board of Methodist Health System, Texas Methodist Foundation, and the Executive Board of Perkins School of Theology at Southern Methodist University. She blogs at www.beyondthebrokenheart.com.